D1275097

GREAT SPORTS TEAMS

THE NEW YORK YANKEES

JOHN F. GRABOWSKI

Lucent Books, San Diego, CA

Library of Congress Cataloging-in-Publication Data

Grabowski, John F.
The New York Yankees / by John F. Grabowski.
p. cm. — (Great sports teams)
Includes bibliographical references and index. (p.).
Summary: Discusses the history of the Yankees baseball team and the lives and careers of players Joe DiMaggio, Lou Gehrig, Mickey Mantle, Reggie Jackson, Derek Jeter, Babe Ruth, and manager Casey Stengel.
ISBN 1-56006-946-5 (hardback : alk. paper)
1. New York Yankees (Baseball team)—History—Juvenile literature. [1. New York Yankees (Baseball team)—History.] I. Title. New York Yankees baseball team. II. Title. III. Series.
GV875.N4 G69 2002
796.357'64'097471—dc21

2001001442

P.O. Box 289011, San Diego, CA 92198-9011
Printed in the U.S.A.

Contents

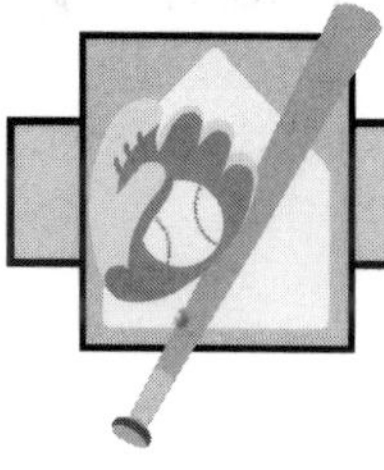

FOREWORD

Former Supreme Court Chief Justice Warren Burger once said he always read the sports section of the newspaper first because it was about humanity's successes, while the front page listed only humanity's failures. Millions of people across the country today would probably agree with Burger's preference for tales of human endurance, record-breaking performances, and feats of athletic prowess. Although these accomplishments are far beyond what most Americans can ever hope to achieve, average people, the fans, do want to affect what happens on the field of play. Thus, their role becomes one of encouragement. They cheer for their favorite players and team and boo the opposition.

ABC Sports president Roone Arledge once attempted to explain the relationship between fan and team. Sport, said Arledge, is "a set of created circumstances—artificial circumstances—set up to frustrate a man in pursuit of a goal. He has to have certain skills to overcome those obstacles—or even to challenge them. And people who don't have those skills cheer him and admire him." Over a period of time, the admirers may develop a rabid—even irrational—allegiance to a particular team. Indeed, the word "fan" itself is derived from the word "fanatic," someone possessed by an excessive and irrational zeal. Sometimes this devotion to a team is because of a favorite player; often it's because of where a person lives, and, occasionally, it's because of a family allegiance to a particular club.

Whatever the reason, the bond formed between team and fan often defies reason. It may be easy to understand the appeal of the New York Yankees, a team that has gone to the World Series an incredible 37 times and won 26 championships, nearly three times as many as any other major league baseball team. It is more difficult, though, to comprehend the fanaticism of Chicago Cubs fans, who faithfully follow the progress of a team that hasn't won a World Series since 1908. Regardless, the Cubs have surpassed the 2 million mark in home attendance in 14 of the last 17 years. In fact, their two highest totals were posted in 1999 and 2000, when the team finished in last place.

Each volume in Lucent's *Great Sports Teams in History* series examines a team that has left its mark on the American sports consciousness. Each book looks at the history and tradition of the club in an attempt to understand its appeal and the loyalty—even passion—of its fans. Each volume also examines the lives and careers of people who played significant roles in the team's history. Players, managers, coaches, and front office executives are represented.

Footnoted quotations help bring the text in each book to life. In addition, all books include an annotated bibliography and a Further Reading list to supply students with sources for conducting additional individual research.

No one volume can hope to explain fully the mystique of the New York Yankees, Boston Celtics, Dallas Cowboys, or Montreal Canadiens. The Lucent *Great Sports Teams in History* series, however, gives interested readers a solid start on the road to understanding the mysterious bond that exists between modern professional sports teams and their devoted followers.

INTRODUCTION

A Tough Team for a Tough Town

New York City is the most exciting, dynamic metropolis in the country, and, arguably, in the world. It is a center of business, finance, entertainment, culture, and almost any other activity one can imagine. With approximately 8 million people living in the greater metropolitan area, competition can be formidable, whether it be for a job, an apartment, or even a parking space. It takes a certain toughness to be successful in New York, a toughness that many people find grating.

New Yorkers expect the same toughness to be shown by their sports teams, the same drive to be number one. To win the hearts of New York's fans, a team must be willing to go the extra mile and do whatever it takes to come out on top. If this means spending more money than the next team, then so be it. Success, it seems, has no budgetary limit.

When it comes to baseball, the New York Yankees epitomize both the drive for and achievement of success. Since moving to New York from Baltimore in 1903, the franchise has produced thirty-seven pennant winners and twenty-six World Series champions. This record is even more remarkable when one considers that the Yankees did not win their first pennant until 1921.

To win an average of nearly one championship every three years over an eighty-year span is an astonishing feat. But such success has naturally produced a degree of resentment among the Yankees' opponents and their fans, since people generally side with the underdog rather than with the team that is favored to win. Moreover, those who side with the Yankees are sometimes thought to be taking the easier path. As sportswriter Jim Murray wrote in 1950, "Rooting for the New York Yankees is like rooting for U.S. Steel."[1]

It takes a tough team to persevere and be successful year after year, decade after decade. In a city in which winning is viewed as almost a birthright, the New York Yankees have proven to be just such a team. They are a dynasty of dynasties, a tough team for a tough town.

CHAPTER 1

The Making of a Dynasty

In 1901, baseball's American League began its first season of play as a major league. The circuit had teams representing Baltimore, Boston, Chicago, Cleveland, Detroit, Milwaukee, Philadelphia, and Washington, but New York was conspicuous by its absence.

The Baltimore Orioles finished in fifth place that maiden season. With the club on its way to a last-place finish the next year, league president Ban Johnson made the decision to relocate the team. Johnson realized the league would have little chance of success without a club situated in the nation's largest city, so the struggling Baltimore franchise would be transferred in order to compete with the New York Giants of the National League.

New Yorkers Frank Farrell and Bill Devery paid $18,000 for the Baltimore franchise. In a rather audacious move, Johnson allowed the club to raid established National League squads in an attempt to sign players who would give it instant credibility. Among those acquired in this way were pitcher Jack Chesbro and outfielder Wee Willie Keeler. Farrell and Devery secured a playing facility on a piece of high land in northern Manhattan—Hilltop Park—despite threats from people with connections to the Giants ("No matter where you go," they were told, "the city will decide to run a street car over second base."[2]) Under the management of former Chicago White Sox player Clark Griffith, the Highlanders—so named because of the location of their home field—prepared to play their first year in New York.

The Highlanders

On April 22, 1903, the Highlanders played their first game, losing to the Washington Senators by a score of 3-1. The contest marked the beginning of a decade that would see the team finish as high as second and as low as eighth. Keeler was their top batter of the period, with Chesbro and Russ Ford having the most success on the mound.

Although the team won its share of games, it was a distant second in the hearts of New Yorkers. The New York Giants, who played their home games in the nearby Polo Grounds, were the better, more exciting team.

But as the new team improved, so, too, did attendance at the Highlanders' games. The club drew twice as many fans in its second season, helping the team stabilize financially. Unfortunately, the improvement in play was not consistent. By 1908 the team had tumbled into the basement. Kid Elberfeld replaced Griffith as manager as the club lost a franchise-record 103 games. Better times lay ahead, however, when George Stallings took over the reins as manager.

In April 1911, the Polo Grounds was demolished by a fire. Highlanders owner Farrell offered the rival Giants the use of Hilltop Park for the remainder of the season and the Giants gladly accepted. Unfortunately, the team's generosity also extended to the playing field. Poor defense combined with weak pitching to drop the Highlanders back into the second division (the bottom half of the eight-team league). The 1912 season ended with New York in last place, a franchise-record fifty-five games behind the pennant-winning Boston club. The sad season saw the team play its last game ever at Hilltop Park.

A Fresh Start

In 1913 the New York Highlanders got a fresh start. They moved into the rebuilt Polo Grounds—a facility far superior to

The New York Yankees, originally named the Highlanders, played at northern Manhattan's Hilltop Park from 1903 until 1913.

Hilltop Park—as tenants of their National League rivals. The Highlanders also got a new name; from then on they would officially be known as the Yankees. The team also took on a new manager, Frank Chance, but continued its unimpressive play.

Disappointed by a dozen seasons of mediocrity, Farrell and Devery sold the Yankees to Col. Jacob Ruppert and Tillinghast Huston in January 1915. The new management hired former star pitcher "Wild Bill" Donovan as manager, and introduced new team uniforms featuring the pinstripes that would make them instantly distinguishable from those of every other team.

The Yankees climbed to fifth place, but posted their worst attendance mark in what would be ten seasons in the Polo Grounds. The fans who did show up saw hints of a change in strategy, with power hitting coming to the fore. The team slugged thirty-one home runs to lead the American League in that category for the first time.

The team continued its slow climb in the standings. The Yankees finished in fourth place in 1918 under new manager Miller

Huggins, and in third the following year. World War I, however, caused attendance to drop as men trooped off to military service in droves. Salaries were cut as management limited the payroll in response to the lost ticket sales. Players found they had no choice but to accept the cuts. "The players can sign at the salaries offered or not at all,"[3] proclaimed Huston. Better times lay ahead, however. They would be ushered in by George Herman (Babe) Ruth, and baseball would never be the same.

The Ruthian Era

On January 3, 1920, the Yankees bought star player Babe Ruth from the Boston Red Sox in a deal that would change the course of baseball history. Ruth dominated the game for the next decade and a half, and the Yankees were the beneficiaries of his success.

Babe Ruth joined the Yankees in 1920, leading the team to its first pennant a year later.

In 1921, Ruth put together one of the greatest seasons in history, leading the Yanks to their first pennant. They won again in 1922, but were defeated in the World Series by the New York Giants both years. Nineteen twenty-three, however, would be a different story.

The year began with the opening of a new home field: Yankee Stadium in the Bronx, which stood across the Harlem River from the Polo Grounds. With a powerful team that included many players acquired from the Red Sox—among them Ruth, Everett Scott, Joe Dugan, Joe Bush, Sam Jones, Waite Hoyt, and Herb Pennock—the Yankees, affectionately dubbed the Bronx Bombers, won the pennant, finishing a whopping sixteen games ahead of the Detroit Tigers. In the World Series that fall, they beat the Giants in six games to win their first world championship.

After dropping to second place in 1924, New York fell all the way to seventh in 1925. Because of his excessive indulgences, Ruth suffered a serious stomach illness that limited him to only ninety-eight games. The pitching staff fell apart, with three of the starters suffering slumps. Nineteen twenty-five also marked the debut of Lou Gehrig and Earle Combs as regular players. Both would play key roles in future Yankee championship clubs. With second baseman Tony Lazzeri added to the mix the next season, New York responded by winning its fourth pennant of the decade. The best, however, was yet to come.

The Greatest Team Ever

The 1927 Yankees club is generally considered the greatest baseball team of all time. The New Yorkers won 110 games and finished 19 games ahead of the second-place Athletics. Ruth clouted a record sixty home runs while Gehrig added forty-seven. The National League champion Pittsburgh Pirates were no match for the Bronx Bombers that year. The Yankees swept 4 straight games to take their second World Series.

Another pennant and World Series sweep (this time over the St. Louis Cardinals) followed the next year. It was, however, manager Miller Huggins's last championship team. The diminutive leader was taken ill in September 1929 and died soon after. His record in twelve seasons at the helm included six pennants and three world championships. His genius lay in his ability to organize a group of talented, unruly players into a smoothly running juggernaut.

Nineteen twenty-nine also marked the introduction of numbers on uniforms, the Yankees becoming the first big league team to wear them. The regular players were given numbers in accordance with their positions in the batting order. From that point on, Ruth and Gehrig were forever associated with the numbers 3 and 4, respectively.

Marse Joe and Joltin' Joe

The year 1930 saw the pitching staff that would dominate the decade begin to take shape as Lefty Gomez was recalled from the minors and Red Ruffing was obtained in a trade from the Red Sox. Hitters were still in control, however: The major leagues introduced a juiced-up baseball designed to provide longer hits to entertain the fans.

In 1931 the Yankees hired former Chicago Cubs manager Joe McCarthy to take over the team. "Marse Joe" had never played in the majors, but certainly knew how to get the best out of his players. Ruth and Gehrig continued their power hitting and New York rose to second place in the standings.

The following year, McCarthy guided the team back to the World Series. New York won 107 games during the regular season, with nine future Hall of Famers dotting the roster. In the series, the Yankees defeated McCarthy's former Cubs team in 4 games straight for the title.

Babe Ruth's departure after the 1934 season saw an end to a ten-year period in which he and Gehrig between them averaged 77 home runs and 274 runs batted in (RBI) per season, and the Yankees' fortunes slipped as a result. It soon became obvious that another power hitter was needed to fill the hole left by the Bambino's retirement. The player who would fill that void—Joe DiMaggio—joined the club as a rookie in 1936.

Sparked by the twenty-one-year-old DiMaggio, the Yankees ran away with the pennant. Joltin' Joe had plenty of help, however. Four other players joined him in driving home at least one hundred runs—Gehrig, second baseman Tony Lazzeri, outfielder George Selkirk, and catcher Bill Dickey. Many who follow baseball consider this team, which defeated the Giants in six games in the World Series, to be second only to the 1927 squad when great teams are discussed.

Nineteen thirty-six marked the beginning of an unprecedented string of four consecutive world

Manager Joe McCarthy led the Yankees in four consecutive world championships from 1936 through 1939.

championship clubs managed by McCarthy. The joy of winning a fourth straight championship in 1939 was tempered by two losses. In January, Col. Jacob Ruppert, the team's owner of twenty-four years, passed away. Several months later, it was revealed that Lou Gehrig—who shortly before had removed himself from the team's lineup—was seriously ill with an incurable neurological disease.

With the loss of Gehrig, 1939 marked the end of a decade of Yankee dominance. Yet the coming years saw the start of another. One third-place finish (1940) was followed by three more pennants and two world championships. The 1941 season featured Joe DiMaggio's remarkable fifty-six-game hitting streak. The team won in 1943 despite the loss of many key players to military service as World War II escalated. In a league populated by teenagers, forty-year-olds, and players who for one reason or another had been rejected for service, the Yankees finished in third place in 1944.

Back from the War

Nineteen forty-five brought a change in ownership to the Yankees, but little change in the team's fortunes. On January 26, Jacob Ruppert's heirs sold the team to Dan Topping and Del Webb, who hired Larry MacPhail as president and gave him one-third interest in the club. With most of the regular players still away in the military, the team finished in fourth place.

The next season saw little improvement. The pressures of the job had been taking their toll on manager McCarthy, who suffered a mild breakdown and was replaced at the helm. Players returning from the armed forces gave the team a needed boost, but few played up to their prewar levels. The club finished the year in third place in the American League. Fan interest was still high, however, and the team's attendance for the season again surpassed the 2 million mark.

With Bucky Harris now managing the team, the Yankees bounced back to win the 1947 pennant by a good margin. One of the highlights of the summer was the club's American League–record nineteen-game winning streak. Buoyed by rookie catcher Yogi Berra and newly acquired pitching ace Allie Reynolds, the club went on to defeat the Brooklyn Dodgers in an exciting World Series.

The victory was especially sweet because of the animosity that existed between the two teams. Former Dodgers coach Charlie Dressen had been lured to the Yankees by former Brooklyn president, Larry MacPhail. Later, Dodgers president Branch Rickey and manager—and former Yankees shortstop—Leo Durocher accused MacPhail of associating with known gamblers at a preseason game. MacPhail denied the accusations and filed a libel suit against Durocher. The Yankees and Dodgers were each fined $2,000 for "engaging in public feuding."[4] The coming years would see the teams develop one of the game's bitterest off-the-field rivalries.

In a surprise move, Harris was fired after leading the team to a third-place finish in 1948. Casey Stengel was hired as his replacement. New York won an exciting pennant race in Stengel's first season in charge, then proceeded to repeat the next four years. In each of those five seasons, they went on to defeat the National League champion in the World Series. The string broke Joe McCarthy's record of four successive championships, and has yet to be duplicated.

When the team was finally defeated in the pennant race in 1954, it took a league-record 111 wins by the Cleveland Indians

Manager Casey Stengel (center) set a new record leading the Yankees to five consecutive championships.

to do so. The Yankees won 103 games that year, setting a record for the highest winning percentage for a second-place team in American League history. The Yankees got back on track again the very next year, winning the first of four consecutive pennants. The streak would give them an incredible run of nine pennants and seven world championships in a ten-year span.

The Yankees won the 1956 pennant easily, as Mickey Mantle won the Triple Crown of baseball (the batting, home run, and runs batted in titles). In the World Series against the Brooklyn Dodgers, pitcher Don Larsen hurled a perfect game as the Yankees won their seventeenth world championship. The series was the last "Subway Series" (so called because the two stadiums where the games were played were just a short subway ride apart) of the century as both the Dodgers and Giants moved to California following the 1957 season.

The final four years of Stengel's term as Yankees manager saw the team win three more pennants (1957, 1958, 1960) and another World Series (1958). When the club lost the 1960 series to the Pittsburgh Pirates, however, Stengel was forced by the Yankees owners to retire.

Continued Success

Former third-string catcher Ralph Houk followed Stengel as manager, and the team he inherited was a powerhouse. The 1961 squad won 109 games and captured their twenty-sixth pennant. Mickey Mantle and Roger Maris (who came to the Yankees in a 1960 trade with the Kansas City Athletics) combined to clout 115 home runs, with Maris's 61 eclipsing Babe Ruth's hallowed single-season mark of 60. As a team, the Yankees stroked a major league record 240 homers that season. By the time the team defeated the Cincinnati Reds in the Series that fall, it had cemented its place among the great teams in baseball history.

Houk continued his magic over the next two seasons, winning two more pennants and another championship (1962). Following the 1963 season, he gave up the managerial position to become the team's general manager. His successor, Yogi Berra, continued the winning tradition by leading the team to its fifth straight pennant the next year.

Off the field, all of baseball was shocked when it was announced in August 1964 that the Columbia Broadcasting Company had bought the Yankees. Despite Berra's winning performance as manager, the team's new owners blamed him when the Yankees lost an exciting seven-game World Series to the St. Louis Cardinals. Berra was relieved of his duties and was replaced, ironically, by Johnny Keane, who had resigned as the Cardinals manager the day after the Series ended.

A Time of Rebuilding

Unfortunately, the job did not turn out to be all that Keane hoped it would be. He inherited a team of aging players whose best years were behind them. The Yankees dropped to sixth place in 1965, the first time they had finished in the second division since 1925.

As bad as 1965 was for Yankees fans, the next year was even worse. Keane was fired after the team won only four of its first twenty games. Ralph Houk came back from the front office to take over the reins.

Houk's second stint as manager was far less successful than his first. The Yankees finished in last place in the ten-team American League, their first time ending up in the cellar since 1912. The team finished higher than fourth only one time in that eight-year period (1970), and compiled losing records in three of those seasons.

Yankees fans were not used to a team that failed to win consistently. The expansion New York Mets of the National League had come on the scene in 1962 and some fans were choosing to attend their games instead. By 1972, Yankee season attendance had dropped to 966,328, the first time since 1945 that the club had failed to draw at least a million fans at home. The drop in attendance proved to be the final straw. CBS entered into negotiations with a group headed by Cleveland shipbuilding magnate George Steinbrenner. The team was sold in January 1973 for approximately $12 million.

The Boss

When he first purchased the team, George Steinbrenner said he would not interfere with the day-to-day operation of the club. "We plan absentee ownership as far as running the Yankees is

George Steinbrenner purchased the Yankees in 1973 and became a very hands-on owner.

concerned," he stated at his first news conference as the club's general partner. "We're not going to pretend to be something we aren't. I'll stick to building ships."[5] His desire to bring New York a winner, however, soon led him to assert his presence more than any previous Yankees owner had done.

Nineteen seventy-six saw the Yankees win their first pennant in twelve years, with the help of several players—such as Ed Figueroa, Dock Ellis, Willie Randolph, Mickey Rivers, and Ken Holtzman—acquired by Steinbrenner via trades. The fans responded by pushing attendance past the 2 million mark for the first time since 1950. First baseman Chris Chambliss's dramatic ninth-inning home run in the final game of the American League Championship Series gave New York the pennant, but the team met Cincinnati's "Big Red Machine" in the Series and was swept in four games.

Never one to be satisfied with anything less than a championship team, Steinbrenner made a bold move by signing free agent Reggie Jackson during the off-season. Jackson helped New York to the 1978 pennant in a thrilling pennant race that saw the Yankees come from fourteen games behind in August to catch the Red Sox and force a one-game playoff for the East Division title. A dramatic home run by shortstop Bucky Dent put New York into the Championship Series against the Kansas City Royals. Reggie Jackson's heroics led the Yankees past the Royals, then on to a World Series win over the Dodgers.

Tragedy struck the team in 1979. All-Star catcher Thurman Munson was killed on August 2 when the twin-engine jet plane he was piloting crashed while he was practicing takeoffs and landings. The team finished in fourth place, in large part due to the loss of their leader, yet still managed to set a new home attendance mark, drawing more than 2.5 million fans.

Those fans were rewarded in 1980 when the club bounced back to take the AL East title. A loss to Kansas City in the League Championship Series prevented them from reaching the World Series, but the team did so in 1981, as free agent outfielder Dave Winfield made his Yankees debut.

The Yankee teams of the 1980s had many great players, but always came up short of a championship. The 1985 team, for example, was marked by constant turmoil and one distraction after another, many of them involving Steinbrenner, who consistently grabbed headlines with his decisions. For example, after telling manager Yogi Berra that he would be with the club all year, Steinbrenner fired the veteran player and manager sixteen games into the season. Steinbrenner sometimes singled out players for criticism, as when he referred to Winfield as "Mr. May," a sarcastic reminder of the outfielder's failure to produce in the 1981 World Series.

Other divisive incidents occurred between team members. Free agent pitcher Ed Whitson beat up Berra's replacement, Billy Martin, after a confrontation in a bar. The manager responded to rumors of his imminent firing with several illogical moves, such as making left-handed batter Mike Pagliarulo bat right-handed against a left-handed pitcher.

The chaos surrounding the team eventually took its toll on the players. They won ninety-seven games during the regular season, but finished two games behind the Toronto Blue Jays. Years later, infielder Graig Nettles would refer to the atmosphere of finger-pointing

Steinbrenner (left) made headlines with his decision to fire manager Yogi Berra (right) only sixteen games into the 1985 season.

and publicized bickering during these years, saying, "Some kids want to run away and join the circus and some kids want to play for the New York Yankees. I got lucky. I got to do both."[6]

Steinbrenner continued to look for big-name players to add to the team, in part for their ability to win and in part for the publicity they could bring the team. "They were trying to win championships," says former vice president of baseball operations Syd Thrift, "and were essentially trading young players for older players. . . . When you're in New York, it's a different problem than anywhere else. You're in a constant battle for media attention with the Mets. No one knew that better than George."[7] The shifting of personnel did not always work to the team's advantage. Some players traded away blossomed after they left the Yankees, including Jay Buhner, Willie McGee, Fred McGriff, Doug Drabek, Al Leiter, J. T. Snow, Otis Nixon, and Jose Rijo. To make matters even worse, the Mets won the championship in 1986, defeating the Boston Red Sox in a memorable World Series. The Mets were the darlings of the city, having overtaken the Yankees in the hearts of the fans and the media.

Back On Track

The Yankees reached a low point in 1990. They finished in last place in the American League East with a record of 67-95, the team's fewest wins since 1918 (except for the strike-shortened season of 1981). Meanwhile, another controversy involving Steinbrenner was brewing. Steinbrenner had hired small-time gambler Howie Spira, and paid him $40,000, to find information that would discredit outfielder Dave Winfield, who had gotten the best of Steinbrenner in contract negotiations. Winfield sued Steinbrenner for failing to make an annual $450,000 contribution to a foundation Winfield had set up. Steinbrenner countersued, charging the foundation with "fraud, wrongdoing and misappropriations."[8] The two sides reached a settlement, but baseball commissioner Fay Vincent permanently barred Steinbrenner from involvement in the everyday operations of the team (later reduced to thirty months), explaining that major league owners "may not pay a gambler for information intended to be used in a dispute involving the owner and a ballplayer."[9]

Upon his return in 1993, Steinbrenner was a changed man. The wholesale hirings and firings stopped. He seemed to understand that the "quick fix" provided by free agents was not the way to build a successful organization. Instead, the foundation had to be built from within, by developing younger players who felt loyalty to the team. He began to build an organization that would develop its own stars.

The team started its long climb back under the leadership of manager Buck Showalter, who guided the club to an East Division championship in 1994. Unfortunately, the season was cut short by a players strike, and postseason play was canceled for the first time since 1904.

Showalter resigned in 1995, in part due to a disagreement with Steinbrenner over the composition of his coaching staff, and was replaced by former Mets manager Joe Torre. Torre brought a measure of calm and confidence that had been missing from the team for years. The players responded in a positive manner.

Owner George Steinbrenner (left) and manager Joe Torre (right) celebrate after the 1998 World Series.

Yankees players are jubilant after defeating the New York Mets to win the 2000 World Series.

In 1996, Torre's first year, the Yankees won ninety-two games (their most since 1985), and their first pennant since 1981. They defeated the Atlanta Braves in the World Series for their first championship in eighteen years.

After a second-place finish the next year, everything came together in 1998. The Yankees won a league-record 114 games in the regular season, barreled past the Texas Rangers and Cleveland Indians in the playoffs, then swept the Atlanta Braves in four games in the World Series. Their 11 postseason victories gave them an all-time record 125 wins for the season, against only 50 losses. Notwithstanding the 1927 team's performance, the 1998 team staked a legitimate claim to the title, "Greatest Team of All Time."

New York continued its dominance in the final two years of the millennium. Although not approaching their incredible record of 1998, the 1999 and 2000 squads also won world championships. The three straight titles made them only the fourth team in history to win that many in a row.

In ninety-eight seasons in New York, the Yankee franchise has won an amazing thirty-seven pennants and twenty-six world championships. No other team has approached that record; the Dodgers' eighteen pennants and the Cardinals' and Athletics' nine championships rank next on the list. It is a record unmatched in sports, and fashioned by some of the greatest players in baseball history.

Chapter 2

Babe Ruth

More than a half-century after his death, Babe Ruth remains arguably the most famous name in the history of American sports. He is generally accepted as the greatest baseball player of all time, excelling as both a hitter and a pitcher. No other player has performed at as high a level in both areas.

But baseball alone does not serve as a measure of the Babe's greatness. Ruth loved people, especially children, and the affection was returned a hundredfold. Fans came out in record numbers to see the beloved Bambino. That he rose to the status of folk hero after spending much of his youth in what many referred to as a reform school makes his story all the more memorable.

More than fifty years after his death, Babe Ruth is still considered the greatest baseball player of all time.

A Young Incorrigible

George Herman Ruth Jr. was born on February 6, 1895, in his grandparents' house in Baltimore, Maryland. His father, a bartender who would later own his own saloon, was of German extraction, as was his mother, Kate Schamberger Ruth, who also worked in the tavern. The couple would have seven other children, but only George and his sister Mary survived to adulthood.

As a youngster, George received little attention from his parents, who were always busy with work. He learned about life on the streets near the Baltimore harbor, and often was truant from school. His escapades were largely harmless, including running around with the older boys, breaking windows, and occasionally engaging in petty larceny.

Unable to supervise George and finding him headstrong and difficult to handle, his parents committed him to St. Mary's Industrial School for Boys when he was just seven years old. The Catholic school was accustomed to such "incorrigible" youths. Some of the boys in the school were orphans, but many were delinquents and runaways.

Each boy at the school was allowed to choose a trade. Ruth decided to be a tailor, and learned how to sew shirts. For each shirt he made, he earned a small amount of money, which he usually spent at the candy store.

At St. Mary's, George came under the guidance of Brother Matthias, a six-foot six-inch giant who was one of the Xaverian Brothers who ran the institution. Brother Matthias gave George the attention and support he had missed at home, and had a profound influence on the lad. "He was the father I needed," said Ruth later. "He taught me to read and write—and he taught me the difference between right and wrong."[10] Brother Matthias also introduced Ruth to baseball. "Ruth played ball the first afternoon he was with us," related Brother Paul, the school's superintendent, "and from then on he played baseball at every opportunity."[11]

Brother Matthias found his new charge had real talent for the sport. George played every position, excelling as a pitcher and hitter.

Shortly after turning nineteen, Ruth was signed to his first professional contract by Jack Dunn, owner of the minor league Baltimore Orioles of the International League. He was to receive $600 for the season. This was also the point at which Ruth earned his nickname. Since Ruth's parents had signed over custody of George to the school, he was supposed to remain there until he was twenty-one. In order to get around this rule, Dunn became George's legal guardian. One of the first times the two appeared together on the field, another player was heard to call out, "There goes Dunnie with his babe."[12]

Ruth made his professional debut as a pitcher on April 22, 1914. He hurled a six-hit shutout against the Buffalo Bisons, getting two hits himself. He exhibited great potential over the next few months, but the Orioles were experiencing financial difficulties. To cut his losses, Dunn sold Ruth to the major league Boston Red Sox. Babe made his major league debut on July 11, pitching his team to a 4-3 win over the Cleveland Indians. After appearing in just five games, he was sent back to the minor leagues for more seasoning—that is, to develop his skills and prepare him for playing in the major leagues. He won twenty-two games in the International League, and rejoined the major leagues for good the following spring.

Success on the Mound

Ruth's first full season with Boston was a rousing success. He won 18 games against only 8 losses for a winning percentage of .692. The Red Sox won the American League pennant, and defeated the Philadelphia Phillies in the World Series. The next year, he won 23 games and led the league in earned run average and shutouts. In Game 2 of the World Series against the Brooklyn Dodgers, Ruth hurled a 14-inning complete game, victory. He also began a streak of 29 consecutive scoreless innings pitched. The Babe was earning a reputation as one of the best pitchers in the game. He boosted that reputation by garnering 24 wins in 1917, the second-highest total in the American League.

Ruth was also demonstrating a skill unusual in a pitcher: He could hit. In 1918 the Red Sox began playing him in the outfield when someone else was pitching, so they could still take advantage

Ruth made his major league debut in 1914 as a pitcher for the Boston Red Sox.

of his powerful bat. Ruth responded by hitting .300, and connecting for eleven home runs to tie for the league lead. He did this while playing in only 95 of his team's 126 games. Ruth also won 13 games as a pitcher in a season shortened due to America's entry into World War I. He led the Red Sox to another championship that fall, defeating the Chicago Cubs twice in the World Series.

Prior to the 1918 season, Ruth had asked owner Frazee to double his salary to $10,000, placing him among the top players of the day. The Boston owner—and New York theatrical promoter—refused to offer more than $7,000. "I've never paid an actor that much,"[13] said Frazee. Frazee did, however, promise him $10,000 for 1919 if he had another good year. Now, with the home run crown in hand, Ruth asked for a three-year contract at $10,000 per season. After a period of negotiations, Frazee gave in to Ruth's demands. The Babe was now earning one of the top salaries in the game.

Playing the outfield more and more in 1919, Ruth put on a batting display that captured the imagination of baseball fans everywhere. He finished the season with what at the time was the unbelievable total of twenty-nine home runs, leading the majors and setting an all-time single-season mark. Philadelphia Phillies outfielder Gavvy Cravath led the National League with twelve, the next highest number.

Despite Ruth's slugging, the Red Sox fell on hard times. They finished in sixth place, and Frazee found himself with money problems. To raise funds, he traded his star attraction to the New York Yankees. Frazee rationalized the trade by saying, "I believe the sale of Ruth will ultimately strengthen the team."[14]

The trade was certainly good for Ruth. Yankees owners Jacob Ruppert and Til Huston gave Babe a contract for $20,000 for 1920. The 225-pound, six-foot two-inch slugger surpassed their wildest dreams. He amassed fifty-four home runs, nearly doubling his record of the previous season. His exploits captivated baseball fans everywhere. In New York, the Yankees now outdrew their crosstown rivals, the New York Giants.

The 1921 season was a memorable one for the Yankees. The club edged out the Cleveland Indians for its first American League pennant. Ruth delivered another home run mark, blasting 59 balls over the fence. He also drove home 171 runs and scored 177, setting a record that would stand into the twenty-first century. The Yankees lost the World Series to the Giants that fall, but through no fault of Ruth's. Babe batted .313, stole a pair of bases, and hit the first of his 15 Series homers, despite being bothered by a boil on his left elbow.

In recognition of his phenomenal season, Ruth asked for—and eventually received—a five-year contract calling for $52,000 per season. When Yankee owner Huston asked him why he insisted on that particular number, Ruth replied, "There are 52 weeks in the year, and I've always wanted to make a grand a week."[15]

Ruth reveled in the attention he received. He lived life to the fullest and did not hesitate to indulge his desires. On more than one occasion, this got him in trouble with the baseball hierarchy. Following the 1921 series, the Babe embarked on a barnstorming tour in which he played in exhibition games, against the wishes of the baseball commissioner. The rule of the day forbade players from World Series teams from appearing in such games reasoning that that would somehow devalue the special impact of the World

Traded to the Yankees in 1920, Ruth soon captivated baseball fans everywhere with his batting skill.

Series. Because of Ruth's defiance, the commissioner suspended him for the first month of the 1922 season.

When Ruth returned in late May, he struggled to catch up with the other players. Perhaps partly out of frustration, he argued with umpire Tom Connolly and was fined by American League president Ban Johnson. He never reached the top of his game, and experienced one of his poorest big league seasons. Still, he batted .315, hit thirty-five home runs, and drove home ninety-nine runs. The Yankees managed to again win the pennant, but were humiliated in the World Series by the Giants, taking just one of five contests.

After the Series, Ruth vowed to change his ways. He kept more active over the winter months, and reported to spring training in the best shape of his career. He was intent on proving that the previous year had been a fluke.

The House That Ruth Built

Despite a season that fell short of expectations, crowds continued to come to see Ruth play. In 1923 the Yankees opened the doors to a new stadium, built to accommodate the fans who came to see the mighty Bambino in action. Yankee Stadium would eventually come to be known as "The House That Ruth Built."

The Babe did not disappoint his fans. On opening day, he slugged the first home run ever hit in the new stadium, then proceeded to hit a career-high .393 for the year. He was named the Most Valuable Player (MVP) of the American League as he led the Yankees to another World Series. He continued his assault in the Fall Classic, as the World Series was known. Ruth batted .368 and hit three home runs as the Yankees defeated the Giants, four games to two. The Yankees were champions for the first time in their history.

Ruth won his only batting title the next season, with a mark of .378. He also hit forty-six home runs to lead the league. The Yankees, however, were beaten out by the Washington Senators to end their string of three straight pennants.

By the time the 1925 campaign began, the Babe had fallen back into his old habits. He lived a larger-than-life existence, enjoying everything to excess, particularly food, drink, and women. The lifestyle finally caught up with him on April 5 when he collapsed in a railroad station. At first, newspaper reports claimed his illness was from overindulging in hot dogs and soda pop, calling it "The Bellyache Heard 'Round the World." But Ruth's illness was later found to be much more serious—what was called an "intestinal abscess"—and required surgery. The result was that Ruth was out of action until the beginning of June. Ruth's excesses had other consequences. Later that summer, he was fined and suspended by Yankees manager Miller Huggins for disobeying team rules. Babe complained to Jacob Ruppert, but the owner stood behind his manager. "Hug fined you because you weren't keeping in shape," said Ruppert, "and we are in back of him 100 percent."[16] Ruth apologized to Huggins and was reinstated. The manager never again had a problem with his star.

Murderers' Row

The Yankees finished the 1925 season in seventh place. Ruth drove home only sixty-six runs as his home run total dipped to twenty-five. By the end of the season, Ruth's weight had ballooned to 265 pounds. He lost the weight, however, and reported to camp for 1926 in top shape. Babe had an extra incentive to do well since the five-year contract he had signed in 1922 was in its last year. A good season would guarantee him a nice raise.

The Bambino's renewed dedication paid off. He hit .372 for the season, with 47 home runs and 145 RBI. The Yanks bounced back from their seventh-place finish of the year before to take the pennant and meet the St. Louis Cardinals in the series. The Yankees lost in seven games, but Ruth thrilled many by slugging three home runs in Game 4.

Ruth received a raise in salary to $70,000 for 1927. He responded with one of the greatest seasons in major league history. The Yankees ran over all opposition, winning 110 games and beating their closest rival, the Philadelphia Athletics, by 19 games. The team led the league in runs scored, triples, home runs, batting average, and slugging percentage (a figure arrived at by dividing total bases by at bats). Ruth was not alone:

In 1927, Lou Gehrig, Ruth, and Tony Lazzeri (left to right) were part of the Yankees regular line-up known as Murderers' Row.

The regular lineup—consisting of center fielder Earle Combs, shortstop Mark Koenig, right fielder Ruth, first baseman Lou Gehrig, left fielder Bob Meusel, second baseman Tony Lazzeri, third baseman Joe Dugan, and catcher Pat Collins—became known as "Murderers' Row."

Ruth's contribution was a new major league record of 60 home runs, together with a .356 batting mark, and 164 runs batted in. Following the regular season, the Yankees swept the National League champion Pittsburgh Pirates in four straight games in the World Series. Ruth batted .400, with a pair of homers included among his six hits.

The Bronx Bombers continued their success the next year, again winning the pennant, this time in a battle that went down to the wire with the Philadelphia Athletics. Ruth reached the fifty-home-run mark for the third time, this time connecting for fifty-four. The World Series again proved to be a mismatch. The Yankees won in four games, this time sweeping the St. Louis Cardinals. Ruth batted .625, the highest mark ever in a single Series. He stroked ten hits, scored nine runs himself and drove in four more. In Game 4, he repeated his feat of 1926 by hitting three home runs in a single game. No other player has ever done so twice in World Series action.

The 1929 season ended on a down note for the Yankees when their manager, Miller Huggins, died near the end of September. Ruth had harbored a dream of someday managing a big league team. He approached Ruppert about the position, but was told, "You're too good a player to have the burden of managing my club."[17] Instead, the job went to former pitcher Bob Shawkey. Babe brushed off the slight and proceeded to bat .359 with another league-leading forty-nine homers. The Yankees, however, dropped to third place behind Philadelphia and Washington.

The "Called Shot"

Shawkey lasted just one year before being replaced by former Chicago Cubs manager Joe McCarthy. This time, Ruth was more upset at being passed over. "I think I have earned a right to get a crack at the job,"[18] he had told Ruppert. The owner disagreed. "For years, Babe," he rejoined, "you couldn't take care of yourself; how can I turn my team over to you?"[19] The decision

Ruth hits another home run.

caused a rift between the manager and his star player that would never completely heal.

The Babe, however, did not let the ill feeling interfere with his job. He batted .373, with 46 homers and 163 runs batted in for 1931, then followed up with a .341 mark, 41 home runs, and 137 RBI the next year. He helped lift the Yankees and McCarthy to the pennant that season. In the Series, the Babe's two homers helped the New Yorkers sweep the Cubs for the title.

Game 3 of the Series was the setting for one of the most famous moments in baseball history. Ruth stepped to the plate in the fifth inning with the scored tied, 4 to 4. After taking two called strikes from pitcher Charlie Root, Ruth raised his hand and pointed toward the center field bleachers. He proceeded to hit the next offering to that exact spot for a home run that gave the Yankees a lead they never relinquished. Ruth never said whether he actually meant to indicate where he would hit that home run, but the incident has become a permanent part of baseball legend.

The Beginning of the End

With the depression at its peak in 1933, Ruth's contract was cut to $52,000. Attendance was dropping, and owners were fearful that fans who were struggling to make ends meet would resent the large salaries given to players. The Babe was thirty-eight and beginning to show signs of wear and tear from years of high living. He still managed to hit .301, clouting 34 home runs in the process. The next year, his production dropped even further. In 125 games, he batted .288, hit 22 homers, and drove home just 84 runs. It would be his last year as a member of the Yankees.

Following the season, Emil Fuchs, president of the Boston Braves of the National League, received permission from Jacob Ruppert to speak to Ruth. Fuchs offered the Babe a contract as a player and vice president, hinting that the job might eventually lead to a managerial position. Ruth knew he would never be the Yankees manager. He was given his release by the Yankees and joined Boston for the 1935 season.

Unfortunately, Ruth had little left to give to his new employer. He hit just .181 in twenty-eight games with the Braves, with one final shining moment. On May 25 he clouted three home runs in a contest against the Pittsburgh Pirates at Forbes Field. The final blast—the 714th and last of his career—cleared the right field seats, carrying well over five hundred feet. One week later, the Babe announced his retirement.

Ruth never did get the opportunity to manage a big league club. He was hired as a coach by the Brooklyn Dodgers in 1938, but that was as close as he ever came. On June 12 of the next year, the Babe was inducted into the Baseball Hall of Fame as a member of its original class.

Ruth wears his uniform for the last time in 1947 when the Yankees retired his jersey number.

On April 27, 1947, the Yankees honored the ailing legend by staging Babe Ruth Day at Yankee Stadium. Two months later they retired his famous Number 3 uniform. Two months after that, the Babe was dead of lung cancer at age fifty-three. Broadcaster Ernie Harwell perhaps best summarized Babe Ruth. "He wasn't a baseball player," said Harwell. "He was a worldwide celebrity, an international star the likes of which baseball has never seen since."[20]

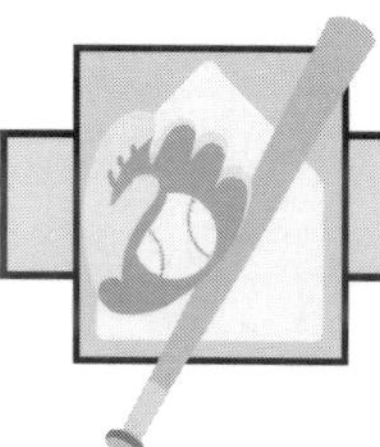

Chapter 3

Lou Gehrig

On June 3, 1932, New York Yankees first baseman Lou Gehrig slugged four consecutive home runs, and narrowly missed a fifth, in the Yankees 20-13 win over the Philadelphia Athletics. The feat had only been turned once before in major league history, by Boston outfielder Bobby Lowe on May 30, 1894.

One would think that such a singular accomplishment would garner headlines in newspapers across the country. Such was not the case, however. It turned out that legendary New York manager John McGraw happened to pick that same day to announce his retirement after thirty-one years at the helm of the Giants. The Gehrig story was forced to take a back seat. In a way, this was appropriate, since playing in the shadow of others was the story of Gehrig's career.

"Lou Lewis"

Heinrich Ludwig (Henry Louis) Gehrig was born on June 19, 1903, in a neighborhood of German immigrants on the Upper East Side of Manhattan. He was the second of four children born to Heinrich and Christina Gehrig, but the only one to survive infancy. Lou's father held a variety of jobs, including those

Lou Gehrig, considered one of baseball's all-time great players, didn't grab headlines like Babe Ruth and Joe DiMaggio.

of handyman, butcher, and janitor. His mother worked as a cook and housekeeper to help the family make ends meet.

As the only surviving child, Lou received all his mother's love and attention. She was devoted to him, and determined to see that his life would be better than hers. She would often take him with her when she went to work; the youngster would sit and play quietly while she performed her duties.

Since he spent so much time with his mother, Lou had little opportunity to make friends. In addition, until the age of five, he only spoke German, as his parents did at home. When he began to learn English in school, he found it much easier to get to know others his age.

One way young Lou was able to communicate with others was through sports. He loved to play all sorts of games, but in hitting a baseball, he excelled. The sport quickly became the boy's first love.

By the time he was a teenager, Lou's skills on the ballfield were evident. He attended the High School of Commerce in New York City, where he was a good student. He made the school's baseball team, and after being tried unsuccessfully in the outfield and as pitcher, found a home at first base. As Lou explained with characteristic humility, "We were mighty short on infielders in those days."[21]

It was at Commerce that Gehrig first came into the public eye and drew a measure of national attention. In 1920 Commerce won the New York City championship, and was invited to go to Chicago to play Lane Tech in a scholastic championship game. Lou hit a grand slam that day to help Commerce to victory. The mighty blast was hit at Wrigley Field, the home of the National League Cubs. "Gehrig's blow would have made any big leaguer proud," wrote the reporter for the *Chicago Tribune,* "yet it was walloped by a boy who hasn't yet started to shave."[22]

Gehrig had also starred as a football player at Commerce, and following his graduation, he attended New York's Columbia University on a football scholarship. The summer before his freshman year, he was offered a spot with the New York Giants Hartford farm team. Giants manager John McGraw advised him to play, but told him to use an assumed name or risk forfeiting his eligibility to play in college. With his father out of work and also needing surgery, Lou knew the money could help his family. Gehrig played under the name Lou Lewis, but was soon found out. He was suspended from playing baseball and football for his freshman year.

Gehrig played football in high school and attended college on a football scholarship.

When Gehrig finally was cleared to play, he impressed everyone with his powerful bat. Yankees scout Paul Krichell was in attendance one spring day in 1923 when Gehrig slugged a massive home run. "I think I've just seen another Babe Ruth,"[23] Krichell told Yankees general manager Ed Barrow. The Yankees signed Gehrig with an offer of a $1,500 signing bonus and a $2,000 contract for the last four months of the 1923 season.

Ironically, Gehrig was sent to Hartford in the Eastern League, which by this time was a Yankees farm team. He played two seasons in the minors, making brief appearances with the big league club at the end of each season. In 1925 he started the season with the major league team.

The Start of Something Big

On June 1, Gehrig pinch-hit for shortstop Pee Wee Wanninger and got a base hit. The next day, Yankees first baseman Wally Pipp complained of a headache. "I don't feel equal to getting back in there,"[24] he told manager Miller Huggins. Huggins inserted Gehrig in his place in the starting lineup. Pipp never regained his job. Day in and day out, year after year, Gehrig could be counted on to take his position on the field, and his swings in the batter's box. Lou Gehrig was a rock they could count on, a player sportswriter Jim Murray would later dub "Gibraltar in cleats."[25]

Gehrig batted .295 as a rookie, with 20 home runs and 68 RBI. In spite of that effort, the Yankees finished in next-to-last place, but prospects for the future looked good. The next year, Lou reached the .300 mark for what would be the first of twelve consecutive seasons. New York bounced back and won the pennant behind the amazing slugging of Babe Ruth. Gehrig produced solid numbers—16 home runs, 107 RBI, and a .313 batting average—but Ruth was the one who grabbed the headlines. It was a pattern that would continue throughout most of the next decade.

Power Personified

In 1927 manager Huggins decided to juggle his batting order. He moved Gehrig into the cleanup position (fourth), behind Ruth and ahead of outfielder Bob Meusel. The trio formed the foundation of a lineup that was christened "Murderers' Row." It was the year that the larger-than-life Ruth crushed the unheard-of total of 60 home runs. Gehrig hit 47 himself, and actually led Ruth as late as mid-August. Ruth's strong finish gave him a new record, overshadowing Gehrig's performance. Lou finished second to the Babe in homers, batted .373, and drove home a major league record 175 runs. For his amazing year, Gehrig was named the American League's Most Valuable Player.

Gehrig followed up with another magnificent year in 1928. He again led the league in RBI, this time with 142. He batted .374, but his homers fell to 27. Still, the Yankees breezed to another pennant, and their second consecutive four-game sweep in the World Series. This Series was a showcase for Gehrig. He batted .545, with 6 hits in 11 at bats. Four of those hits were home runs. Lou drove in 9 runs, scored 5, and compiled an incredible slugging percentage of 1.727.

Over the next few years, Ruth and Gehrig carried the Yankees, forming the most devastating one-two batting punch in the history of the game. Gehrig was the model of consistency, a run-making machine, but was often on the fringe of the spotlight surrounding Ruth. Lou understood and accepted this fact of life, realizing everyone else fell in the Babe's shadow. "It's a pretty big shadow," he said. "It gives me lots of room to spread myself. . . . Let's face it, I'm not a headline guy. I always knew that as long as I was following Babe to the plate, I could have gone up there and stood on my head. No one would have noticed the difference."[26]

Not even Ruth, however, could match Gehrig's consistency. Lou played game after game, never missing a day no matter what the circumstances. He played through bumps and bruises, and

Even though he had considerable talent of his own, Gehrig (left) understood and accepted that he played in the shadow of the great Babe Ruth (right).

also through more disabling conditions, like a broken thumb, a broken toe, and a painful, chronic inflammation of the tendons and muscles of the lower back. Gehrig never complained, winning the respect and admiration of teammates and fans alike.

After what was, for him, a subpar year in 1929, Gehrig put together a string of the greatest seasons anyone has ever had. It began with a career-high .379 average in 1930, with 41 homers and 174 runs batted in. The next year, he batted .341, with 46 home runs, and a new American League record of 184 RBI. He also led the league in hits (211) and runs scored (163).

An incident that occurred early that season caused Gehrig to be robbed of a home run title he rightfully should have won outright. On April 26 he hit a drive into the center field stands in Washington. The ball bounced back onto the field, and was caught by Senators outfielder Sam Rice. Yankees runner Lyn Lary saw the ball being caught and thought it was the final out of the inning. As Lary headed for the dugout, Gehrig continued to round the bases on his homer and was called out for passing his teammate on the basepaths. Lary's base-running blunder cost Lou a homer and two runs batted in. He was credited with a triple, and finished the year in a tie with Ruth for the home run crown, rather than winning it outright.

In 1932, Gehrig batted .349, with 34 more homers and 151 runs batted in. The Yankees captured their first pennant under Joe McCarthy, who had taken over the reins of the team the year before. That fall, the club swept the Cubs in the Series. Gehrig hit .529, clouted 3 home runs, drove home 8 runs, and scored 9 himself.

The Iron Horse

On August 17, 1933, the St. Louis Browns defeated the Yankees, 7-6, in a ten-inning contest. Of more significance than the score was the fact that the game was Gehrig's 1,308th in a row. With it, he surpassed Everett Scott's all-time mark for consecutive games played. He had appeared in every game the Yankees had played for more than eight years. As incredible as the mark was, Gehrig was not yet ready to take a rest. He continued to pound the ball, batting .334 for the year, with 32 home runs, 139 RBI, and a league-leading 138 runs scored.

In August 1933, Gehrig accepted a trophy in recognition of his record-breaking 1,308 consecutive games played.

The following year saw Lou continue his assault on the record books. On May 10, despite being ill with a severe head cold, he stroked two home runs and a pair of doubles to tie the record for "long" hits in a game. He knocked in seven runs in the contest, a full day's work by anybody's standard. Incredibly, Gehrig performed the feat in just five innings. Illness forced him to sit out the rest of the game.

At the end of the season, Gehrig's name was at the top of the three major batting categories. He led the American League in batting average (.363), home runs (49), and runs batted in (165), becoming just the fourth player in American League history to win baseball's Triple Crown.

In 1935, Gehrig batted .329, hit 30 homers, drove in 119 runs, and scored a league-leading 132. The Yankees could not overtake Detroit, however, and the Tigers won their second consecutive American League crown. It became obvious that Gehrig could not carry the team all by himself. New York needed another powerful bat in the lineup to put them back on top of the American League standings.

A New Dynasty

A young outfielder by the name of Joe DiMaggio joined the team in 1936, and proved to be just what the Yankees needed. His mighty bat and all-around play sparked the team to its first pennant since 1932. Gehrig, of course, was his usual magnificent, consistent self. He batted .354, with a league-high 49 home runs and 152 runs batted in. He also led the league in runs scored and slugging percentage. He played every game, of course, and his playing streak passed the 1,700-game mark. For his efforts, Lou was again named the American League's Most Valuable Player.

The dynamic, young DiMaggio began to garner more and more attention while the quiet, unassuming Gehrig again fell into the shadow of a more charismatic teammate. He quietly went about his business, which in 1937 was helping the Yankees win yet another World Series.

A Fatal Disease

The 1938 season was Gehrig's last full year with the Yankees. His production began to fall as he batted under .300 for the first time since his rookie year. His home run and RBI totals were also short of what Yankee fans had come to expect from him. The New Yorkers won their third consecutive championship, but there was a change in Gehrig's play. At long last, it seemed as though age and the playing streak (now standing at more than 2,100 games) were catching up to the "Iron Horse." Because of Gehrig's standing as a respected leader of the team, however, McCarthy would not even consider sitting him down. "That's Lou's decision,"[27] said the manager.

By the spring of 1939, it was obvious to the players and writers who covered the team that something was wrong with

Gehrig. Joe Williams of the *New York Telegram* wrote, "On eyewitness testimony alone, the verdict must be that of a battle-scarred veteran falling apart."[28] The six-foot, two-hundred-pound slugger was ineffectual at the plate and had no range in the field. On the bases, as teammate Tommy Henrich remembered, "It looked like he was trying to run uphill."[29]

Gehrig began the year in the regular lineup, but struggled badly at the plate. His batting average was well below .200 seven games into the season. In the next game, against the Washington Senators, Lou went hitless in four at bats. The last play of the game was a ground ball back to the mound. Yankees pitcher Johnny Murphy handled the ball and tossed to Gehrig for the final out. Trying to encourage his teammate, Murphy congratulated him as he walked off the field. Gehrig knew better. He realized his play was hurting the team. He knew it was time to step aside.

The next day, Gehrig told manager Joe McCarthy to put someone else in his place. McCarthy had Gehrig bring the lineup card out to the umpires before the game. Babe Dahlgren's name was listed at first base. "Ladies and gentlemen," proclaimed the announcer, "Lou Gehrig's consecutive streak of 2,130 games played has ended."[30]

Gehrig checked himself into the Mayo Clinic, where he was examined by a team of doctors. He was diagnosed with amyotrophic lateral sclerosis (ALS), a rare degenerative disease of the central nervous system. His baseball playing days were over. On July 4, 1939, the Yankees held Lou Gehrig Appreciation Day to honor their stricken hero. New York City mayor Fiorello H. La Guardia officially thanked Lou for his services. "You are the greatest prototype of good sportsmanship and citizenship. Lou, we're proud of you."[31]

More than sixty-two thousand fans filled the stands at Yankee Stadium as Gehrig strode to the microphone. "Fans," he began, addressing the throng, "for the past two weeks you have been reading about the bad break I got. Yet today I consider myself the luckiest man on the face of this earth." By the time he finished, there wasn't a dry eye in the stadium. Gehrig closed by saying, "I may have had a tough break, but I have an awful lot to live for."[32]

Gehrig stands with head bowed as he is honored on Lou Gehrig Appreciation Day, July 4, 1939.

The new Baseball Hall of Fame in Cooperstown, New York, waived the waiting period required for membership and Gehrig was admitted in 1939, the year it opened. The Yankees officially retired his uniform number, the first time a major league team had honored a player in this way.

For the last two years of his life, Gehrig worked on youth projects for New York mayor La Guardia. On June 2, 1941, he died in Riverdale, New York, less than three weeks before his thirty-eighth birthday, and exactly sixteen years to the day after he had replaced Wally Pipp at first base in the Yankees lineup. As a measure of his fame, from that day on ALS has been commonly known as Lou Gehrig's disease.

Gehrig died in 1941 at the age of thirty-seven.

By any definition, Lou Gehrig was one of baseball's all-time great players. As a person, however, he stood even taller. His grace and quiet dignity in the face of adversity serve as a model for young and old alike. He was truly an all-American hero whose legacy will be remembered as long as the game of baseball is played.

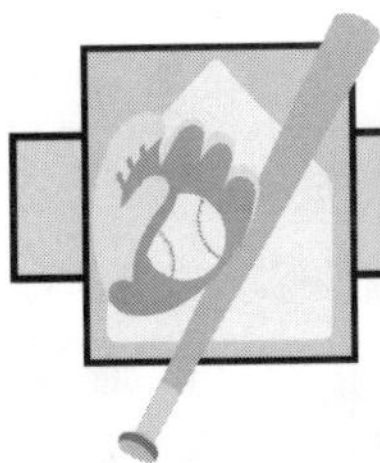

Chapter 4

Joe DiMaggio

For the last decades of his life, whenever Joe DiMaggio was introduced to an audience, his name was prefaced by the phrase "the greatest living ballplayer." It was hard for anyone to argue with that appellation. As former Los Angeles manager Tommy Lasorda once said, "If you said to God, 'Create someone who was what a baseball player should be,' God would have created Joe DiMaggio. And he did."[33]

Growing Up in the City by the Bay

Joseph Paul DiMaggio Jr. was born in Martinez, California, some twenty-five miles northeast of San Francisco, on November 25, 1914. He was the fourth of five sons, and eighth of nine children born to Giuseppe and Rosalie DiMaggio. Giuseppe was a fisherman who moved his family to the North Beach area of San Francisco when Joe was an infant. Two of the sons would follow their father in his profession; three would become major league baseball players.

As a youngster, Joe was very active in sports. Like his older brother Vince, he began playing baseball at an early age, in part to get away from the chores associated with fishing. His talent

Joe DiMaggio smashes a home run in June 1939.

soon showed, and by the time he was a teenager, he had made a name for himself in the area by starring for a local semipro team.

School did not play a major role in his life. Joe got through Hancock Elementary and Francisco Junior High with passing grades. Exceedingly quiet, afraid of giving a wrong answer and *appearing* dumb, he rarely answered questions.

At Galileo High School, he missed classes on a regular basis. He eventually got caught and received a beating from his brothers. The school showed little interest in keeping him as a student, however, and he finally dropped out for good. He got a job stacking wooden crates, then another as a laborer in an orange juice plant. It was baseball, however, that was his true passion.

Through Vince, Joe got his first chance to play baseball for money. Vince had signed a contract with the San Francisco Seals of the Pacific Coast League. One day in 1932, Joe was watching the team play and was offered a chance to work out with the club by Seals president Charley Graham. Based on what Graham saw, DiMaggio was invited to play in the last three games of the season at shortstop. He stroked a triple off veteran Ted Pillette in his first at bat, and was impressive enough to be invited to training camp the next spring. At that time, Joe was signed to a contract that called for him to receive $225 a month. He began the season on the bench, together with his brother Vince. When he got his chance to play he made the best of it.

Although signed as a shortstop, Joe was switched to the outfield, where his strong arm would be particularly useful. At his new position, the eighteen-year-old pounded Pacific Coast League pitching for a .340 average. At one point during the season, he set an all-time professional record by hitting safely in an incredible sixty-one straight games, a mark that has lasted nearly seven decades. The streak brought Joe to the nation's attention. "Baseball didn't really get into my blood until I knocked off that hitting streak," he would later say. "Getting a daily hit became more important to me than eating, drinking, or sleeping. Overnight, I became a personality."[34] The streak attracted scouts from all the major league teams.

Joe followed up the 1933 season by batting .341 the next year, but he also suffered a knee injury that almost put an end to his career. Joe's knee buckled while he was getting out of a cab. The diagnosis was torn ligaments, and he was forced to keep his leg in a cast for six weeks. The injury frightened away fifteen of the teams that had shown interest in him. The Yankees, however, decided to take a chance. It was agreed that he would play the next season with the Seals, then report to the Yankees in 1936.

New York, New York

DiMaggio impressed everyone in the Yankees organization with his smooth style right from the beginning of spring training in 1936. First baseman Lou Gehrig told writers, "I predict that in three years, DiMaggio will be ranked with the greatest right-handed batsmen of all time. Joe exemplifies the utmost in conservation of energy. There's no hitch in his style."[35]

After missing the first two weeks of the season with a sore right foot, DiMaggio made his debut against the St. Louis Browns on May 3. In his first major league game, he belted two singles and a triple in six trips to the plate. For the year, Joe batted .323 while hitting 29 home runs and driving home 125 runs.

The Yankee team Joe joined had not won a pennant since 1932. DiMaggio's power was just what the club needed, helping them take the American League by storm. Unlike the great majority of rookies, he did not appear to have any major weaknesses. Sportswriter Jimmy Cannon noted, "There was nothing they could teach Joe D. When he came to the big leagues, it was all there."[36] As far as his prowess as a runner was concerned, there was none better. "He never made one mistake on the bases," said former manager Joe McCarthy. "If he went for an extra base, he made it."[37]

He helped the New Yorkers win the pennant by a whopping margin of nineteen and a half games. The Yankees went on to defeat the New York Giants in six games in the World Series, as Joe stroked nine hits and batted .346. DiMaggio's contribution to the team's success was obvious to everyone. After the Series, Giants manager Bill Terry said, "I've always heard that one player could make a difference between a losing team and a winner, and I never believed it. Now, I know it's true."[38]

DiMaggio was even better in 1937. He surpassed his totals in

The Yankees took a chance on twenty-two-year-old DiMaggio, who joined the club in 1936.

every major category, stroking a career-high 46 homers, with 167 RBI and 151 runs scored, while batting .346. Again, thanks to DiMaggio's hitting, New York won the World Series by defeating the Giants.

Believing himself to be undervalued, DiMaggio held out prior to the start of the 1938 season, asking for more money. Yankees owner Jacob Ruppert stood fast, however, and after a couple of weeks, Joe signed for $25,000. DiMaggio came to regret having made money an issue. He was booed by fans throughout the season for his perceived greed, and as a result, promised never again to hold out from signing a contract.

With the controversy over his salary demands behind him, DiMaggio added to his totals over the next two years. In 1939 he won the first of his three Most Valuable Player awards, leading the Yankees to their fourth consecutive pennant and fourth straight world championship. He won back-to-back batting titles in 1939 and 1940 with averages of .381 and .352, respectively. All the personal glory was secondary to Joe, who had vowed to put the team's interests ahead of his own, and so 1940 was a disappointment since New York finished in third place, behind the Detroit Tigers and Cleveland Indians.

The Streak

Despite all his individual totals, however, no one could have predicted what DiMaggio would accomplish the next season. What DiMaggio did from May 15 through July 16 of 1941 has become a part of baseball lore. Over that two-month stretch, he batted safely in every one of his team's games. Day after day, Joe ripped one hit after another. People all across the country watched with interest, whether or not they were Yankee fans. The streak even made its way into song. Bandleader Les Brown's arrangement of "Joltin' Joe DiMaggio" became a hit tune all across the country.

DiMaggio tied the old mark of 44 consecutive games, set by Willie Keeler in 1897, then racked up a dozen more. Joe stroked 91 hits over that period, belted 15 homers, drove in 55 runs, and batted .408. Incredibly, he struck out only 7 times.

On July 17, a record 67,468 fans packed Cleveland's Municipal Stadium to see the Yankees play the hometown Indians. Joe was held hitless by Cleveland pitchers Al Smith and Jim Bagby, as Indians third baseman Ken Keltner made two sterling plays to rob him of hits. The streak was finally over. Afterward, DiMaggio was characteristically humble, saying, "Of course I wanted to go on as long as I could. Now that the streak is over, I just want to get out there and keep helping to win ballgames."[39] And that is exactly what he did. Incredibly, DiMaggio got a hit the next day, and batted safely in the next sixteen games. He had come within a hairbreadth of hitting in seventy-three straight contests.

The fifty-six-game streak is cited by many as one of baseball's most unbreakable records. None other than baseball great Ted Williams proclaimed, "I believe there isn't a record in the books that will be harder to break. [DiMaggio's hitting streak] may be the greatest batting achievement of all."[40] It assured DiMaggio of his place as one of the legends of the game.

Red Sox player Ted Williams (left) was one of many who believed DiMaggio's incredible 1941 batting streak would never be broken.

The War Takes Its Toll

Despite his success on the field, physical and personal setbacks began to wear on DiMaggio in 1942. He had married a young actress named Dorothy Arnold following the 1939 season, but after the birth of his only child, Joe Jr., in late 1941, the marriage began to unravel. The stress from the marital problems affected his health, and Joe developed ulcers the next summer when his wife moved out. The effect of the breakup could also be seen in his performance on the field. Although New York won yet another pennant in 1942, DiMaggio posted his poorest statistics to date in batting average, home runs, and runs batted in. That fall, the Yankees lost the World Series for the first and only time in DiMaggio's career, dropping a five-game set to the National League champion St. Louis Cardinals.

DiMaggio's breakup with wife Dorothy Arnold in 1942 hurt his performance on the playing field.

Potentially more damaging to DiMaggio's career was his decision, as World War II was intensifying, to enlist in the Army Air Force in January 1943. By the time he made his next appearance on a major league baseball field, three prime years of his career were gone. (So, too, was his wife, who after a brief reconciliation filed for divorce in October 1943.)

Joe was discharged from military service in late 1945, and returned to the Yankees the next season. The effects of his time away from baseball were evident. He batted just .290 his first season back, with 25 home runs and 95 runs batted in. Although most players would have loved to have put up those numbers, it was the poorest season of his career.

Joe rebounded in 1947. Despite problems with a heel spur and bone chips in his elbow, he compiled a .315 batting average, with 20 homers and 97 RBI. Although not up to his prewar standards, the figures earned DiMaggio his third Most Valuable Player award as he carried the Yankees to another pennant and world championship. The next year gave fans a glimpse of the old Joe DiMaggio. "Joltin' Joe" raised his average to .320, and led the American League in both home runs and runs batted in.

Joe was again hobbled by injuries in 1949. Bone spurs in his right heel caused him to miss the first half of the year, but then the pain in his heel miraculously disappeared in late June. He joined the Yankees in Boston on June 28, when they began a three-game series against the powerful Red Sox. Joe made headlines by leading his team to a crucial three-game sweep. He clouted 4 homers and drove home 9 runs in the series, and the Yankees were on their way to yet another pennant and world championship. In DiMaggio's half-season of work, he compiled a .346 batting average, 14 home runs, and 57 RBI.

Following his 1948 heroics, DiMaggio had been rewarded with a $100,000 contract for 1949, the first player ever to reach that magic figure. Despite his slowly eroding performance, he was still worth every penny. In 1950 he batted .301, slugged 32 homers, drove in 122 runs, topped the league with a slugging percentage of .583, and led the Yankees to yet another pennant and World Series championship.

Despite his heroics, the thirty-five-year-old outfielder knew he was nearing the end of his playing days. When training camp got underway the next spring, Joe had reached a decision—the 1951 season would be his last. Many fans did not believe him. They were confident he would be lured back by the promise of another $100,000 contract. Joe, however, remained true to his word. As he later explained, "I didn't think I could give them a $100,000 year."[41]

DiMaggio ended his major league career in winning fashion. The Yankees won the World Series again in 1951, their ninth championship in DiMaggio's thirteen seasons. Joe struggled, finishing with a career-worst .263 average, just 12 home runs and 71 RBI. He took the field for the last time in Game 6, two days after having hit his eighth World Series homer to help win Game 4. In his last at bat, DiMaggio stroked a double off the right center field wall in the eighth inning, ending his career a winner.

Joe and Marilyn

Retirement did not stop DiMaggio from making headlines though. In late 1951 he was introduced to Hollywood's hottest actress, Marilyn Monroe, and the two began dating. Millions of Americans wanted this fairy-tale romance to work, and the couple believed they were made for each other. "I was surprised to be so crazy about Joe," Marilyn told a friend. "He treated me like something special. Joe is a very decent man, and he makes other people feel decent, too."[42]

A little more than two years later, on January 14, 1954, Joe and Marilyn were wed. They spent their honeymoon in Japan and Korea, where Marilyn was entertaining American troops. During her appearances, she was greeted with rousing ovations by servicemen. "Joe," Marilyn reportedly told him, "there were a hundred thousand people there and they were all cheering and clapping; you've never heard anything like it." "Yes I have,"[43] replied Joe quietly.

Joe loved Marilyn, but hated the extravagant Hollywood lifestyle and the constant

DiMaggio divorced his second wife, Marilyn Monroe, after just nine months.

media attention. Moreover, DiMaggio and Monroe soon found their personalities were at odds. He was an introvert who liked to stay home and watch television. Marilyn was an extrovert who needed to be showered with attention. Under the stress of their divergent needs, the marriage soon fell apart. Joe and Marilyn were divorced just nine months after they were wed, on October 27. What the media had called the Romance of the Century was over.

Although they found that marriage to each other did not suit them, Marilyn and Joe remained on friendly terms until Monroe's death in 1962. Joe made all the funeral arrangements for his ex-wife. As he knelt by her casket, he kissed her cheek and whispered, "I love you. I love you."[44] For the next twenty years, DiMaggio religiously sent roses to her grave three times a week.

An American Icon

The fact that his marriage to Marilyn Monroe failed did not diminish DiMaggio's luster as a celebrity, particularly in baseball circles. Joe DiMaggio was voted into the Baseball Hall of Fame in 1955. Surprisingly, this was his third year of eligibility. Several voters reportedly had withheld their votes the first two years because they believed he would come out of retirement and play again.

The honors kept piling up. In 1969 baseball celebrated its centennial and as part of the festivities, sportswriters honored the top players from the game's first one hundred years. In a special vote, DiMaggio was named baseball's greatest living player. DiMaggio was humble as he acknowledged the honor with humor. "At my age, I'm just happy to be named the greatest living anything."[45] He became baseball's ambassador, appearing at charity events and other public forums. In his role as a living legend, he made annual appearances at the Yankees old-timers game each summer. He also remained active in major league baseball, serving as a coach and executive vice president with the Oakland Athletics for two years. Corporate America also took advantage of DiMaggio's fame; new generations came to know him as the television spokesman for Mr. Coffee.

DiMaggio takes a closer look at his Hall of Fame plaque in 1955. The baseball icon continued to receive numerous honors until his death in 1999.

DiMaggio continued to find satisfaction in charitable efforts. One of his greatest pleasures was working for the Joe DiMaggio Children's Hospital in Hollywood, Florida. Over the years, he helped raise thousands of dollars for the institution, helping hundreds of children through his efforts.

On September 27, 1998, Joe made his last appearance at Yankee Stadium. Yankees owner George Steinbrenner acknowledged DiMaggio's contribution to baseball and to the Yankees, saying, "Joe DiMaggio is a national institution and he is a living symbol of the pride, class, and dignity which are synonymous with the Yankee pinstripes."[46]

Shortly after this appearance, DiMaggio fell ill and was hospitalized. He was diagnosed with inoperable lung cancer. On

March 8, 1999, Joltin' Joe DiMaggio, the Yankee Clipper, died at the age of eighty-four.

On April 23, 1999, at a memorial service, New York City mayor Rudolph Giuliani addressed those who had gathered at St. Patrick's Cathedral to honor the Yankee great. His words echoed the thoughts of all those who had followed DiMaggio through the years. "The man who was called the greatest living ballplayer will live forever in the hearts and minds of all New Yorkers," said the mayor. "He graced our city with nine World Championships, but more important than that, he graced our city with a style and a dignity and a class that made New York City better than it actually is."[47]

Chapter 5

Casey Stengel

Luckily for Major League Baseball, most dentists around the turn of the century were right-handed. Had that not been the case, the game might well have been deprived of one of its most colorful personalities—Casey Stengel.

Stengel was a player, coach, and manager in the major leagues, and a storyteller par excellence. He was baseball's greatest goodwill ambassador, willing to talk to anyone, anytime about the game that was his consuming passion. His legacy of quips, stories, and pranks still brings smiles to faces today, more than a quarter century after his death.

Casey Stengel was involved in professional baseball for more than fifty years as a player, coach, manager, and goodwill ambassador.

Dentistry's Loss

Charles Dillon Stengel was born in Kansas City, Missouri, the third child of Louis and Jennie Stengel, a German insurance salesman and his Irish wife. The oldest child, a girl named Louise, was born in 1886, and the next, son Grant, one year later. Charles, the youngest, came along on July 30, 1890. Louis provided a comfortable life for his family. The Stengels always lived in a roomy house with a big yard in which the children could play.

Charley, as the youngest, was his mother's favorite. He was a mischievous youngster who usually hung out with his older brother. The two became close friends, with sports as a common bond.

Charley struggled in school. As was a common practice of the day, his first-grade teacher made the left-handed Charley write with his right hand. The difficulties he encountered doing this were likely a factor in his falling behind in his studies.

Charley and his brother both excelled at sports. They occasionally played football and basketball, but baseball was their favorite. By the time he was ten years old, Charley was playing with boys who were much older. He was a powerfully built, aggressive player who could hit well, throw hard, and run fast.

At Kansas City Central High School, Charley was an all-around athlete. He was the star of the school's basketball team, which won the city championship in 1909. That spring, he pitched the baseball team to the state championship. At the same time, he was also playing semipro ball for a team known as the Kansas City Red Sox. This experience gave Stengel a taste of the rowdy life enjoyed by the ballplayers of the day, a life perfectly suited to the fun-loving youngster.

Stengel's talent as a ballplayer made him known throughout the region. While in his last year at Central, he was offered a contract for $135 a month from the Kansas City Blues of the American Association, a minor league team just one step below the majors. Stengel decided he could not pass up the opportunity or the money. He signed with the Blues and left school a couple of credits short of graduating.

Because of his potent bat, the Blues soon switched Stengel

from pitcher to the outfield. He was farmed out to Kankakee, Illinois, and then Shelbyville, Kentucky, to learn the finer points of playing his new position.

Stengel struggled at the beginning of his professional career and decided to cover himself for the future. Dentistry at the time was a profession one could enter even without a high school diploma, and Casey enrolled in Western Dental College in Kansas City during the off-season. Later, Stengel claimed he had problems learning dentistry because his instructors were right-handed. As Casey once described his skills as a dentist, "I was not very good at pulling teeth, but my mother loved my work."[48]

Stengel quit dental school after two years and turned his attention solely to baseball. His skills on the field improved, and he attracted the eye of Larry Sutton, a scout for the Brooklyn Dodgers. The Dodgers drafted Stengel and sent him to Montgomery, Alabama, for the 1912 season. He batted .290 for the year and was brought up to the major leagues in September.

Stengel's big league debut was one to remember. Brooklyn manager Bill Dahlen inserted him in center field, hitting second in the batting order against the visiting Pittsburgh Pirates. Batting against twenty-four-game winner Claude Hendrix, Stengel got four singles and a walk. The speedy outfielder also stole two bases and scored a pair of runs in Brooklyn's 7-3 victory. At the time, no one had ever had more hits in a major league debut. Playing regularly for the remainder of the season, Stengel compiled a .316 batting average.

Becoming Casey

The scrappy twenty-two-year-old began the next year as Brooklyn's regular center fielder. He got off to a fast start, but suffered an ankle injury that kept him out of action for a month. Manager Dahlen noticed that Stengel's production at the plate was much greater against right-handed pitchers. When the young outfielder returned from the injury, Dahlen began using another player in his position when left-handed pitchers opposed the team. During this period, Stengel acquired a new nickname. Because of his constant references to his hometown of Kansas City, his teammates began calling him "K.C." This soon evolved into "Casey."

Stengel began his professional baseball career with the Brooklyn Dodgers in 1912.

Casey Stengel spent fourteen years in the majors as a player with the Dodgers, Pirates, Phillies, Giants, and Braves. He batted .284 for his career, with a total of 60 home runs in 1,277 games. In 1922, his most productive season, he hit .368 for the New York Giants of John McGraw. His success carried over into postseason play. He batted .393 in twelve World Series games with the Dodgers and Giants, stroking 2 home runs and driving home 4 runners. Both homers were game-winning blasts for the Giants in the 1923 Fall Classic against the New York Yankees.

As good as he was as a player, Casey garnered as much publicity for his antics as for his ball-playing talents. He was a showman through and through, playing the game he loved with a passion but treating it with irreverence. Some called him an overage juvenile delinquent, and he later admitted to having gone a bit too far on more than one occasion. "Now that I am a manager," he later said, "I see the error of my youthful ways. If any player ever pulled that stuff on me now, I would probably fine his ears off."[49]

Perhaps Stengel's most fabled prank took place during the 1919 season. The previous year, he had been traded by the Dodgers to the Pirates. Returning to Brooklyn's Ebbets Field, Casey was being taunted mercilessly by the Dodger fans. As he marched to the plate to a chorus of catcalls, he grandly turned to the crowd, bowed, and tipped his hat, releasing a small sparrow that he had captured and stashed there. The fans howled with glee. Casey, they realized, had just "given them the bird."

Another time, a fellow Dodger was the victim of a Stengel prank. As a publicity stunt, former Dodgers manager Wilbert Robinson planned to catch a baseball dropped from an airplane. Robinson circled under the sphere as it came down to earth, unaware that Stengel had substituted a ripe grapefruit for the baseball. As Casey later related, "Robbie got under this grapefruit, thinking it was a baseball, which hit him right on this pitcher's glove he put on and the insides of it flew all over, seeds on his face and uniform, and flipped him right over on his back. Everybody came running up and commenced laughing, all except Robbie."[50]

Stengel's reputation as a prankster and clown became more of an asset after his playing days in the major leagues were over. Following the 1925 season, Boston Braves owner Judge Emil Fuchs hired Stengel as president, manager, and right fielder of the club's minor league team in Worcester, Massachusetts. Fuchs knew Casey could still hit, and as a headline name, he would undoubtedly draw many fans to games.

Stengel began developing his managerial talents and learning the business side of baseball. Part of the job was handling the media and the fans. He discovered that by acting the part of the buffoon, he was able to draw attention away from his less-than-stellar players. Of those, he had more than his fair share, so in seven seasons as a minor league manager, his clubs won only one pennant.

That period of Stengel's life was far from a total loss, however. In 1924 he married Edna Lawson, an accountant and former actress. Together, they established a residence in Glendale, California. It would serve as their base of operations for the next forty years.

Back to the Majors

Despite his lack of success as a manager, Stengel found himself back in the major leagues in 1932, this time as a coach with the Brooklyn Dodgers. New Brooklyn manager Max Carey had been a teammate of Stengel's on the Pittsburgh Pirates in 1918 and 1919, and helped convince the Brooklyn management to hire him. Two years later, Stengel took over as manager when Carey himself was fired. The team continued to struggle, and after three years Stengel was let go, his club never having finished higher than fifth place. Although Stengel did a credible job of helping develop many younger players, he couldn't shake his reputation as a clown.

Stengel fared no better with the Boston Braves (temporarily renamed the Bees from 1936 to 1940), who hired him as their manager in 1938. In 1943, his last season at the helm, he suffered a broken leg after being struck by a taxi in Boston. Having grown tired of Stengel's shenanigans, a local newspaper sarcastically nominated the cabdriver as its sportsman of the year. "The man who did the most for baseball in Boston was the motorist who ran down Stengel and kept him away from the Braves for two months,"[51] read the column. Casey was fired soon after, and it appeared that at age fifty-three, his career was over.

Such was not the case, however. After spending some time at home recuperating from his injury, Stengel returned to manage in the minor leagues as a favor to his friend, Charlie Grimm. Grimm was manager and part owner of the minor league Mil-

Stengel served as manager of the Boston Braves from 1938 to 1943.

waukee Brewers. Grimm had been offered the job as manager of the Chicago Cubs, but needed to find someone he could trust to take over the reins of the Brewers and protect his interest in the team. He turned to his old friend Stengel, who brought the team home in first place.

Stengel left Milwaukee after the season, hoping to land another job with a major league team. When nothing turned up, however, he accepted George Weiss's offer to manage the Kansas City Blues—the New York Yankees American Association farm team. He was forced out after one year when the major league club was sold. Stengel accepted a position as manager of the Oakland Oaks of the Pacific Coast League in 1946, in part because he made his home in California. He remained at Oakland for three years, guiding his team to the postseason playoffs each season. After winning the pennant in 1948, the *Sporting News* named him its minor league manager of the year.

Stengel's success at Oakland did not go unnoticed in New York. When the Yankees fired manager Bucky Harris following the 1948 season, they hired Stengel as his successor. He was in the majors once again.

Success in the Big City

At a press conference following his hiring, Stengel joked about his qualifications for the job. "This is a big job, fellows," he said, "and I barely have had time to study it. In fact, I scarcely know where I am at."[52] Many people agreed with him. They thought he had been hired in order to draw attention away from what many figured was a subpar Yankees team. Casey eventually addressed his critics. "I know I can make people laugh," he said, "and some of you think I'm a damn fool, [but] I got the job because the people here think I can produce for them."[53]

Stengel silenced criticism that very first year at the helm. The Yankees had finished in third place in 1948, behind the Boston Red Sox and Cleveland Indians. In 1949 they were faced with a flood of injuries, including one to outfielder Joe DiMaggio that forced the perennial all-star to miss half the season. Despite these handicaps, Stengel used his roster masterfully. He juggled his lineup daily to get the best performance from players who hit well against particular pitchers, and took advantage of each player's individual talents. When the Yankees defeated the Red Sox in the final two games of the season, New York had itself another pennant winner.

The Yankees' opponent in the World Series was Casey's old club, the Brooklyn Dodgers. New York defeated Brooklyn in five games, giving them the world championship in Stengel's first season in the American League. The victory was especially sweet for the man most people had considered a failure in the minors. Typically humble about his own contribution, Stengel was effusive in praise of his players. "This is the greatest ball club a man could manage," said Stengel. "A really great bunch of fellows and I am indebted to them for the way they came through for me. They won it. Not me."[54]

In each of the next four seasons, Stengel again led his team to the top of the baseball world. The Yankees won the World Series each year—beating the Phillies in 1950, the Giants in 1951, and the Dodgers in 1952 and 1953—to give them an unprecedented five consecutive championships. With this last victory, Stengel broke the record of four in a row set by former Yankees manager Joe McCarthy.

Casey accomplished this unprecedented feat with a simple philosophy toward managing. Rather than use just eight regular players on a day-in, day-out basis, he platooned at several positions, meaning that the players who he thought would do best against a particular opponent would be his starters that day. As a result, players competed against each other for playing time, bringing out the best in each. Some players did not like this arrangement, but none could argue with the results.

Yankees manager Stengel (center) poses in 1952 with members of his pennant-winning team (from left to right: Yogi Berra, Allie Reynolds, Phil Rizzuto, and Gil McDougald).

Stengel's winning streak was broken in 1954, but through no fault of his own. That year, he led the Yankees to 103 victories, the most they would win in his tenure with the team. The Cleveland Indians, however, won an incredible 111 games, setting an American League record in the process.

New York bounced back to take the pennant the next year, although they lost the Series to the Dodgers. They also won pennants in 1956, 1957, and 1958, winning two more championships as well. Stengel's Yankees were edged out for the American League crown in 1959 by the Chicago White Sox, but won again in 1960, in what would be Stengel's last year as the Yankees skipper.

That year, there was grumbling among some of the players that Stengel's magic was gone. According to them, many of the moves he made were questionable. Some intimated that he had become grouchier with age, alienating many of the younger players with his sarcastic criticism. Others went so far as to hint that the old man (he had turned seventy in July) was becoming senile, and occasionally fell asleep on the bench during games. Yankees president Dan Topping, who had never been a Stengel fan, decided it was time to do something.

That fall, the Yankees faced the Pittsburgh Pirates in the World Series. Although they outscored the Pittsburgh club by a margin of 55 to 27, New York lost the Series on Bill Mazeroski's dramatic home run in the bottom half of the ninth inning of Game 7. Five days later, on October 18, the Yankees held a press conference to announce that Stengel had "retired" as manager. Casey's pride would not allow him to hold his tongue, and he aired his belief that his age was being held against him. "I was fired,"[55] Stengel told reporters. "I'll never make the mistake of being seventy again."[56] Soon afterward, Yankees general manager George Weiss, Stengel's good friend and the man responsible for signing him as manager, was also let go. New York, however, had not seen the last of the duo.

The Amazin' Mets

New York had been without a major league team in the National League since 1958 when the Giants and Dodgers moved to California. In order to remedy the situation, a group headed by former Dodgers president Branch Rickey began formulating plans for a new major league. This new circuit, to be called the Continental League, was to include a team in the city. With the threat of competition on the horizon, the National and American Leagues, each added two teams. New York was awarded one of the new franchises by the National League, to begin play in 1962, and the New York Mets were born.

Mrs. Charles Shipman Payson, the owner of the new team, hired George Weiss as club president. Weiss, in turn, hired Stengel to be the club's first manager. The rationale for the move was simple. A new team could not possibly be competitive for several years. New York fans, accustomed to rooting for winners, would likely favor the powerful Yankees over the newcomers. Something else was needed to attract attention to the team. That something would be the charismatic Stengel.

Stengel was the perfect choice for the job. The 1962 Mets were one of the worst teams in major league history, winning only 40 games while losing 120. With Casey's help, however, the club gained legions of fans who sympathized with their plight. The fans knew the club was doomed to failure because of the quality of player they were given by the established teams. "Look at him," quipped Casey about one of his men. "He can't hit, he can't run, and he can't throw. That's why they gave him to us."[57]

Stengel drew attention to himself with his unique style of double-talk, fractured syntax, and rambling sermons, called "Stengelese" by sportswriters. He talked to everyone and anyone who would listen. He promoted his "Amazin' Mets" everywhere he went, and the team grew in popularity, despite the fact that they would win just fifty-one and fifty-three games over the next two seasons.

Casey Stengel's career with the Mets was cut short when on July 24, 1965, following a party at famed restaurateur Toots Shor's establishment, he fell and broke his left hip. An artificial joint was surgically inserted in place of the damaged one. Several weeks later, however, when it became obvious he would be unable to return to his regular managing duties, Casey retired. Stengel was made a vice president with the Mets, and became the supervisor of scouting in California. The position was largely honorary, however, and he was not a major factor in the team's management.

In March 1966, the team asked him to come to spring training to take part in a ceremony, although he was not given details of its nature. He arrived to find that the Baseball Writers Association of America had agreed to waive the rules requiring a person to be out of baseball for five years before he could be inducted into the Hall of Fame, in order to allow Stengel entry. At the induction ceremonies that summer, Casey rambled on in classic Stengelese. "I want to thank my parents for letting me play baseball," he told the crowd, "and I'm thankful I had baseball knuckles and couldn't become a dentist."[58]

Stengel remained involved in baseball well into his eighties. Every year, he would attend spring training with the Mets in Florida, as well as take part in the Hall of Fame weekend in Cooperstown, the old-timers game in New York, and the World Series. His energy never flagged, even as his ability to move around diminished.

Stengel eventually retired to his home in Glendale, where he lived on the money supplied by baseball and his shrewd investments. For the last year of his life, he tended to his wife, Edna, who had been disabled by a series of strokes.

Old age began to get the best of Stengel. Appearing in New York for the Mets old-timers game in June 1975, he rambled on and on, almost incoherently. His physical frailty was obvious to all. That September, he entered Glendale Memorial Hospital, apparently for a checkup. Doctors found he had developed an incurable form of lymphatic

Stengel remained involved with the game he loved until his death in 1975.

cancer. On September 29, 1975, he died there at the age of eighty-five.

Stengel left the game he loved with 1,905 wins and 1,842 losses as a manager. In spite of this nearly even win-loss record, he won ten pennants, tying him with John McGraw for the most in major league history. His biggest contribution to baseball, however, was spreading his love of the game to all he met. As former Mets outfielder Richie Ashburn said at Stengel's funeral, "Don't shed any tears for Casey. He wouldn't want you to. He loved life and he loved laughter. He loved people and above all, he loved baseball. He was the happiest man I've ever seen."[59]

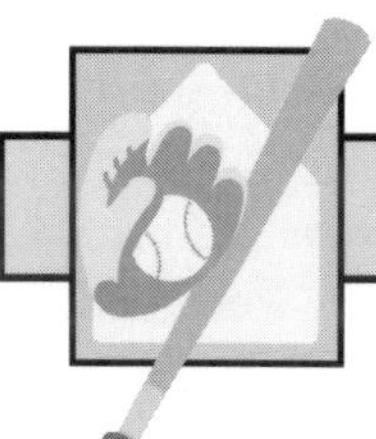

Chapter 6

Mickey Mantle

When Joe DiMaggio played his final season with the Yankees in 1951, one of his teammates was a nineteen-year-old slugger by the name of Mickey Mantle. In many ways, they were very different. DiMaggio was the noble aristocrat, untouchable and aloof. He oozed dignity and class, and guarded his privacy from the prying eyes of an adoring public. Mantle was the wide-eyed country boy who was always eager to join teammates for a night out on the town.

Their careers overlapped that one season, the veteran bowing out gracefully and the rookie trying to establish himself in the big city. That one season was enough, however, to give observers a hint of things to come. The baton had been passed. The Yankees of Joe DiMaggio would become the Yankees of Mickey Mantle. Another glorious chapter in the team's history was about to be written.

The Commerce Comet

Mickey Charles Mantle was born in Spavinaw, Oklahoma, on October 20, 1931. He was the oldest son of Elvin "Mutt" Mantle and his wife, Lovell. The Mantles had three other sons—Butch and the twins, Ray and Roy—and a daughter, Barbara. Mutt Mantle was an avid baseball fan. He named his son after his favorite player, Detroit Tigers Hall of Fame catcher Mickey Cochrane.

Mutt worked in the zinc and lead mines six days a week, and played semipro baseball on Sundays. He didn't want his son to have to work in the mines, and thought baseball would be a way to a better life. Whenever he had free time, he spent it teaching Mickey the finer points of the game of baseball. From the very beginning, he encouraged Mickey to learn the art of switch-hitting. By doing so, he would never be at a disadvantage, since right-handed batters generally hit better against left-handed

Sluggers Joe DiMaggio (left) and Mickey Mantle (right) played only one season together; DiMaggio's final season with the Yankees was Mantle's first.

pitchers, and vice versa. Mantle later recalled, "He believed that any kid could develop into a switch-hitter if you taught him early enough."[60] Baseball was the common bond that helped forge a loving relationship between the father and son.

By the time Mantle was twelve years old, he could see that his father was in ill health. After spending eight hours a day underground in the mines, he would cough and wheeze continually from the dust he had inhaled. Mutt assumed he would die young, either from Hodgkin's disease, which had killed two of his brothers and his father, or from tuberculosis. Consequently, his philosophy was to live every day as it came, not worrying about the future. It was a philosophy Mickey himself would embrace.

When Mickey was still a youngster, the Mantles moved to a farm in Commerce, Oklahoma, to escape the mines. Unfortunately, a torrential rain flooded the area, and everything was lost. The family was forced to move into a little shack in the village of Whitebird on the edge of Commerce. It was a hard time for Mickey's father, who realized he would have to return to work in the hated mines.

Mantle's talent for sports began to show at Commerce High School, where he starred in baseball and football. It was there that he earned the nickname "The Commerce Comet." While in high school, he suffered an injury that almost ended his career before it had a chance to begin. One day, during football practice, Mantle was kicked in the shin, an injury that developed into osteomyelitis, an inflammation of the bone marrow. At one point, doctors spoke of the possibility of amputation. Luckily, medication improved the condition, although the osteomyelitis never completely left him.

Mickey's big chance came when New York Yankees scout Tom Greenwade came to Oklahoma to scout some prospects for the team. One of these was the third baseman on Mantle's team, but Mantle caught his eye by slugging a pair of long home runs. Greenwade realized Mantle's talent was something special. "The first time I saw Mantle," he later recalled, "I knew how [Yankees scout] Paul Krichell felt when he first saw Lou Gehrig. He knew that as a scout, he'd never have another moment like it."[61] Upon Mickey's graduation from high school,

Greenwade signed him to a contract calling for a $1,100 bonus and a salary of $400 a month.

A Phenom

The youngster was assigned to the Independence club of the Class D Kansas-Oklahoma-Missouri League. He impressed everyone immediately, batting .313 that first year as a seventeen-year-old "phenom." His fielding, however, left much to be desired. He was uncertain in handling ground balls, and his throws were erratic. In eighty-nine games at shortstop, Mantle committed forty-seven errors.

The errors did not discourage the Yankees, who were enamored by his ability to hit a baseball. In 1950, Mantle moved up to Class C Joplin of the Western Association. There he pounded the ball at a .383 clip, while stroking 26 homers and driving home 136 runs. The Yankees were pleased with his progress and invited him to a special "instructional school" to be held prior to spring training the next year.

Mickey Mantle was discovered by a Yankee scout who was impressed with the young man's ability at bat.

Mantle impressed Yankees manager Casey Stengel in spring training, and he started the 1951 season with the major league club. "He should lead the league in everything," said Stengel. "With his combination of speed and power, he should win the triple batting crown every year. In fact, he should do everything he wants to do."[62]

There turned out to be one thing, however, that he could not do. As minor league manager Harry Craft reported, "He can run, steal bases, throw, hit for average, and hit with power like I've never seen. Just don't put him at shortstop."[63] In two seasons, Mantle had committed more than one hundred errors. The Yankees installed Mantle in right field, alongside Joe DiMaggio.

The powerful young nineteen-year-old was in the opening day lineup for New York on April 18 against the Boston Red Sox. After going hitless in his first two at bats, Mantle singled home a run his next time up with his first major league hit. In a game against the Chicago White Sox on May 1, he gave a hint as to his potential by blasting a long home run off Randy Gumpert. In general, however, Mantle was clearly overmatched by big league pitching. On July 15 he was sent down to the Yankees' minor league farm team in Kansas City for more seasoning.

The youngster took the demotion hard. He continued to struggle at Kansas City, and began to question his own ability. One day he called his father to tell him he was thinking of quitting. Mutt came to meet him at his hotel and showed Mickey no sympathy. "You're a quitter," he said. "I'm taking you home. You can go to work in the mines."[64]

Mutt's response shook Mickey. He knew he didn't want to work in the mines of Oklahoma, which had taken so much out of his father. Mantle rediscovered his batting stroke, and proceeded to tear up the league. He batted a robust .361, hitting 11 homers and driving home 50 runs in only 40 games. He was back with the Yankees that August, in time for the last few weeks of the season.

New York edged the Cleveland Indians for the pennant and played the New York Giants in the World Series. Mantle started in right field for the Yanks, and batted leadoff. What should have been a joyous occasion for the youngster turned out to be one of the worst of his life, however.

In the fifth inning of Game 2 at Yankee Stadium, Giants rookie center fielder Willie Mays hit a fly ball to right-center field. Mantle and DiMaggio both took off after it. In the course of his pursuit, Mickey's foot caught in a drainage outlet in the outfield, and he went down in a heap. He was carried off the field on a stretcher with torn cartilage in his knee. Surgeons largely repaired the damage, but his knee would continue to bother him.

The day after the accident, there was more bad news, this time of a personal nature. Mutt Mantle had been taken ill. He was eventually diagnosed with Hodgkin's disease. Mutt Mantle would die at age thirty-nine before the next season began. He would never see his son become the star he dreamed he could be.

Hints of Greatness

The first couple years of Mantle's major league career saw him compile solid numbers, though not the spectacular ones many had predicted for him. From 1952 through 1955, his batting averages were .311, .295, .300, and .306. His home runs peaked at a league-leading thirty-seven in 1955, while his high in runs batted in was 102 in 1954.

In spite of recurring pain in his knee, Mickey had become known for his blazing speed. Batting from the left side, he had been timed running to first base in a remarkable 3.1 seconds. That speed was also a valuable asset when patrolling the vast reaches of center field in Yankee Stadium.

Of course Mantle also had the ability to drive five-hundred-foot home runs from both sides of the plate. One of his earliest blasts occurred in Washington's Griffith Stadium in 1953. Batting right-handed against Senators pitcher Chuck Stobbs, Mantle hit a tremendous shot over the left-center-field wall. "I never saw a ball hit so far," marveled Yankees pitcher Bob Kuzava. "You could have cut it up into fifteen singles."[65] After the game, Yankees publicity director Arthur "Red" Patterson paced off the distance from home plate to the spot where the ball had landed, in the backyard of a nearby home. It had traveled an astonishing 565 feet.

Mantle had become a solid, consistent performer. Not until 1956, however, did Mickey show what he was capable of achieving. On May 30, the Yankees played a doubleheader at home against the Washington Senators. With Mantle at the plate in the second game, Washington pitcher Pedro Ramos tried to slip a fastball by him. Mantle connected, and the ball rose majestically toward the right-field stands. It kept on going until finally hitting the right-field roof, just a foot or so from the top. Mantle had come within a few inches of becoming the first person to hit a fair

Thanks to his father's instruction, Mantle could switch-hit and smash home runs from either side of the plate.

ball out of Yankee Stadium. It was estimated that the ball would have traveled more than 600 feet had it not hit the roof. The home run was Mantle's twentieth of the season, making him the first player to ever hit that many before June.

Mickey continued to pound the ball all year. Fans and writers speculated whether this would be the year that Babe Ruth's single-season home run record would be broken. Such was not to be the case, however. Following a September slump, Mantle finished with 52 home runs to go along with a .353 batting average and a career-high 130 runs batted in. All three were league-leading marks, giving Mantle the Triple Crown. After hitting three more homers in the Yankees' World Series win over the Brooklyn Dodgers, he was named the American League's Most Valuable Player. The *Sporting News* named him its major league player of the year, and he was awarded the Hickock Belt by the National Sportswriters Association as the professional athlete of the year.

In 1956, baseball fans wondered if Mantle would break Babe Ruth's single-season home run record.

Mantle followed up with another magnificent season in 1957. Again he won the MVP award, batting a career-best .365, hitting 34 homers, and driving in 94 runs. That fall, however, he suffered another injury in the World Series against the Milwaukee Braves. While leading off second base in the first inning of Game 3, Mantle dove back in to avoid a pickoff attempt. Milwaukee second baseman Red Schoendienst dove for the ball and landed on Mickey's right shoulder. Mantle remained in the game, and later even hit a home run. The shoulder stiffened up that night, however, and the injury would continue to bother him, off and on, for several years.

Over the next three seasons, Mantle continued to produce solid numbers, despite a variety of nagging injuries. In his first ten years in the majors, he led New York to eight pennants and five world championships. He was not Joe DiMaggio, however. Many Yankee fans idolized the Yankee Clipper, who, to them, symbolized everything a ballplayer should be. Mantle was more fallible than the regal Joe D. Some resented the youngster simply for replacing DiMaggio; others focused on his strikeouts and failures. Fans' attitudes toward Mantle, though, would begin to change in 1961.

The Great Home Run Race

In December 1959, the Yankees had obtained outfielder Roger Maris in a trade with the Kansas City Athletics. With a swing perfectly suited for the short right-field wall at Yankee Stadium, Maris began to develop into a home run hitter. In 1960, he had edged Mantle for the American League's Most Valuable Player award in the second-closest vote ever. Maris powered 39 home runs, drove home a league-leading 112 runs, and batted .283. Mantle recorded a .275 average, with 40 homers and 94 RBI. The M&M boys, as they became known, led the Yankees to yet another World Series, where they were upset by Pittsburgh.

Yankees manager Ralph Houk noticed a change in Mantle during spring training of 1961. "He's a man now," said Houk. "Mature. I think his mind's at ease and it shows in the way he plays.... He's in better shape this year than he has been during the spring for a long time.... He could have another year like 1956."[66] The Yankees started out slowly, but soon picked up steam. Mantle and

The M&M boys, Mantle (left) and Roger Maris (right), led the Yankees to the World Series in 1961 and battled each other to break Babe Ruth's single-season home run record.

Maris were hitting home runs at a record pace. By midseason it appeared as if either, or both, could break Ruth's record.

The race soon brought the difference between Mantle and Maris into sharp focus. As the pressure of the chase for the record mounted, Maris became more and more withdrawn. He disliked the constant media attention and it showed. Mantle, on the other hand, seemed unfazed, and clearly became the fans' favorite. If anyone was to break the mighty Bambino's sacred mark, Mantle, who never complained while playing through one injury after another, was the people's choice.

As it turned out, an infection resulting from a flu shot in early September short-circuited Mickey's run. He finished with

54 homers, while Maris went on to hit 61 to set a new standard. Maris could not surpass Mantle in popularity, however. From that point on, "the Mick" could do no wrong in the eyes of the fans.

The Later Years

In recognition of his outstanding performance, Mantle was given a contract for $82,000 for 1962. Only Joe DiMaggio had ever earned more in pinstripes. The money did not have a negative effect, and 1962 was another solid year for Mantle. His .321 batting average, 30 home runs, and 89 runs batted in earned him a third Most Valuable Player award, and the Yankees yet another world championship.

By this time, the assorted injuries of the past decade had begun to take their toll. So, too, had years of partying and carousing. Having lost several relatives to Hodgkin's disease, Mantle fully expected to die young as well. In later years he would say, "If I knew I'd live this long, I would have taken better care of myself."[67]

In June 1963, Mantle fractured a bone in his left foot when he ran into a chain-link fence during a game in Baltimore. The cartilage in his knee was also damaged, and he missed a good part of the season. With Mickey appearing in only sixty-five games, the Yankees still managed to win the pennant, but were swept in four games by the Dodgers in the World Series.

The following year was Mantle's last big season. At age thirty-two, he seemed comfortable in the role of team leader, though many of his old teammates had either retired or been traded away, and a new group of players surrounded him in the clubhouse. Mantle had already accomplished a great deal. He would now lead the youngsters to one final title. Mickey batted .303, clouted 35 home runs, and drove in 111 runs. Under new manager Yogi Berra, New York made it to the World Series for the twelfth and final time in Mantle's eighteen-year career. It took seven games, but the Yankees were defeated in the Fall Classic by the St. Louis Cardinals, despite three home runs and eight RBI from Mantle.

In the final four years of his career, Mickey was but a shell of his former self. One injury after another wracked his body and his batting average gradually dropped, reaching .237 in 1968. He didn't complain, but his limp was a constant reminder of his pain to those who watched him. "He's hurting worse than ever," said former teammate John Blanchard, "but he won't admit it."[68]

The Yankees' fortunes mirrored Mantle's. In each of the years from 1965 to 1968, they finished at least twenty games out of first place. The team's lack of success ate away at Mantle. As teammate Whitey Ford said, "That's what Mickey was all about—winning. Nobody cared more about winning, and nobody took losing harder."[69] Mantle knew the end was in sight for his time as a player.

Mickey Mantle played his last game with the Yankees in 1968.

Mickey Mantle played his last game with the Yankees in 1968. The following March, he announced his retirement. "I can't play any more," he explained. "I can't hit the ball when I need to. I can't steal second when I need to. I can't go from first to third when I need to. I can't score from second when I need to. I have to quit."[70]

Over the years, Mantle had battled back from numerous injuries that would have kept most other athletes on the sidelines. He overcame the aches and pains to hit 536 home runs in a magnificent career. His place among the legends of the game was cemented in 1974 when he was voted into the Baseball Hall of Fame in Cooperstown on the first ballot.

The Toughest Battle of All

Mantle's biggest battle of all, however, was still to come. Mickey had never had a drink until his father died. Devastated by the elder Mantle's death, he had turned to alcohol, hoping to forget his loss. With the Yankees, he enjoyed partying with his teammates, particularly best friends Billy Martin and Whitey Ford. "If I hadn't met those two at the start of my career," he would recall with a grin, "I would have lasted another five years."[71] After his retirement, his drinking continued. In early 1994, he checked himself into the Betty Ford Center, a well-known clinic for treating addiction.

He knew his drinking had hurt his relationship with Merlyn, his wife of forty-two years, and his sons, Mickey Jr., David, Danny, and Billy. Hoping he might help others by making his problem known, Mantle publicly announced his alcoholism. Unfortunately, years of drinking had done irreparable damage to his liver. In June 1995 he received a liver transplant. During the surgery, doctors discovered an inoperable cancer lesion. On October 13, 1995, Mantle died of liver cancer at the age of sixty-three.

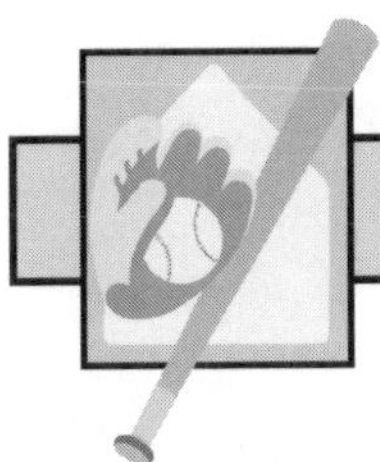

CHAPTER 7

Reggie Jackson

In a career that spanned twenty-one major league seasons, Reggie Jackson spent only five years with the New York Yankees. Most people, however, will always associate him with the Bronx Bombers. The self-proclaimed "straw that stirs the drink"[72] was a perfect match for the town that was the media center of the country. Like New York itself, Jackson was brash, arrogant, boastful, charming, and demanding. Also like the city, he was never dull.

From Pennsylvania to Arizona to California

Reginald Martinez Jackson was born in Wyncote, Pennsylvania, on May 18, 1946. The rest of his family included his father, Martinez Clarence Jackson, his mother, Clara, two children—Joe and Dolores—from Martinez's previous marriage, Reggie's brother James, and his sisters Beverly and Tina.

The Jacksons owned a two-story house on Greenwood Avenue in Wyncote. Reggie's father ran a tailoring and cleaning business on the first floor, and the family lived upstairs. The family was

Reggie Jackson spent only five years with the Yankees even though his professional baseball career spanned twenty-one major league seasons.

poor by most standards but Reggie's parents always made sure there was food on the table.

Reggie remembered his parents often fighting when he was a child. When the boy was six years old, his mother and father separated. Clara Jackson left with her other three children, while Reggie stayed with his father, together with Joe and Dolores. Reggie's father was tough on him and passed along his values. Martinez Jackson taught Reggie to appreciate what he had, and to value and take care of his possessions.

Jackson's talent for sports became obvious at a young age. He inherited some of his ability from his father, who had played ball with the Newark Eagles of the old Negro League in the 1920s and 1930s. At age thirteen, Reggie was the star player on the Greater Glenside Youth Club baseball team.

At this time he first experienced racial prejudice. Each year, the GGYC team would play an all-star series—called the Dixie Series—against a team from Fort Lauderdale, Florida. Reggie, who had grown up and gotten along with youngsters of all races, was the only black on the team. When it came time for the Dixie Series, Reggie's coach would not let him play against the Florida kids. His father tried to explain that prejudice was something Reggie would have to face as he grew older, but it was a bitter lesson for a thirteen-year-old to have to learn.

Jackson attended Cheltenham Township High School, where he was a football, baseball, basketball, and track star. Through his participation in athletics, Reggie was able to release and channel some of the anger that had built up inside him since his parents' separation, particularly in football, which was his best sport.

One day during his senior year, he came home from school to find police cars in front of his house. The stunned seventeen-year-old learned that his father had been arrested for making bootleg corn liquor in a still in the basement of the house. Reggie, of course, had known about the still, but considered it a harmless way for his father to bring a little extra money into the house. He had no idea that it could lead to his father's arrest. Martinez was sentenced to six months in jail, and Reggie was more alone than ever. He and his brother took care of the shop until his father's release. In the meantime, Reggie graduated high school and received a football scholarship to Arizona State University.

"I Was Raw"

During his freshman year, Jackson tried out for the school's baseball team. Reggie had speed and power, but had to refine his baseball skills. "I had a lot of talent and a lot of ability," he would later say. "But I was raw. I hadn't played baseball much; I was a football player. I knew I could hit the ball far. I could run and throw. But I was a raw baseball talent, feeling his way around the game."[73] He refined that talent in short order, under the tutelage of Arizona coaching legend Bobby Winkles.

As a sophomore, Jackson carried the Sun Devils to a 41-11 record, while leading the team in most offensive categories. He made the All-America squad, and was the second player chosen in the 1966 amateur draft. Had it not been for a regrettable miscalculation on the part of the New York Mets, Jackson quite likely would have begun his major league career in the Big Apple. Having the first overall pick in the 1966 amateur draft, the Mets passed on Jackson and instead selected catcher Steve Chilcott. The Kansas City Athletics took Jackson with the next pick.

Jackson signed with the Kansas City team for $85,000 and was assigned to their Class A farm team in Lewiston, Idaho. He moved up to Modesto that same season, then jumped to Birmingham of the Southern League in 1967.

Jackson made his major league debut in June of that year, but did not become the A's regular right fielder until the following season, by which time the team had moved to Oakland. Reggie clouted twenty-nine home runs in his rookie year, helping owner Charlie Finley's club jump four positions in the standings to finish in sixth place. Even in this first year in the major leagues, Jackson was recognized as having value both on and off the field. As veteran second baseman Dick Green said, "Reggie was the first superstar in Oakland. He could carry a team with his bat and take the pressure off his teammates with his mouth."[74]

In 1969 the National and American leagues each separated into two six-team divisions for purposes of determining who would play for the pennant. Oakland gave the Minnesota Twins competition for the West title before finishing second. Despite a late-season slump, Jackson stroked 47 home runs, two behind Minnesota's Harmon Killebrew for the league lead. Reggie impressed even himself when he hit a homer. "These guys [today] hit their home runs," said teammate Vida Blue, "then stand there and watch it. I think Reggie started that, admiring his home runs, then going into his own unique jog around the bases. It's showboating, but it's entertaining."[75]

The A's finished second again in 1970, then blew the competition away the next year. Vida Blue, Catfish Hunter, and Rollie Fingers led Oakland's pitching staff, while Jackson's thirty-two homers powered the offense. The team finished sixteen games ahead of the Kansas City Royals. In the All-Star Game in Detroit, Jackson hit one of the longest home runs in the history of Tiger Stadium, a blast that would have cleared the right-field roof had it not hit a light tower.

Jackson spent his rookie season with the Oakland A's and his twenty-nine home runs that year helped the team advance four positions in the standings.

The A's fell to the Baltimore Orioles in the American League Championship Series that fall, but made it to the World Series in 1972. There, they defeated the Cincinnati Reds in seven games. Unfortunately, Reggie missed the Series due to a pulled hamstring suffered playing against Baltimore.

The following season was one of Jackson's best. He led the American League in runs scored, home runs, runs batted in, and slugging average. For his performance, he was named the league's Most Valuable Player. Oakland finished first in the West, defeated the Orioles in the League Championship Series, then polished off the New York Mets in another seven-game World Series for their second consecutive championship. Jackson drove home six runs against New York to pace the team, and added the Series MVP trophy to his collection.

The A's were a brash, confident, talented, but independent-minded group. They would fight among themselves, then go out and whip the opposing team. No one exemplified these qualities more than Jackson. In one confrontation in June 1974, Jackson squared off against fellow outfielder Bill North. Reggie injured his shoulder in the skirmish, while catcher Ray Fosse suffered a crushed disk in his neck attempting to separate the pair.

Despite the injuries, Oakland continued its winning ways. The A's won their third straight title that year, this time defeating the Los Angeles Dodgers in five games. The victory put the A's in select company. Only the 1936–1939 Yankees and 1949–1953 Yankees had ever won as many as three consecutive titles.

The Oakland dominance would not last, however, as the team's members began to go their separate ways.

After another West Division crown in 1975, Finley, who was suffering severe financial troubles, began to break up his team in order to reduce his payroll. Jackson was traded to the Baltimore Orioles. Reggie helped that team to a second-place finish with a solid all-around season that included a career-high twenty-eight stolen bases.

The lure of the big city was something Jackson could not ignore, however. Taking advantage of the new rules of the day, he filed for free agency after the 1976 season. Jackson followed his former teammate, Catfish Hunter, and signed a five-year contract with the New York Yankees. Reggie loved being in the spotlight and New York was the perfect stage for him. Anticipating great things, he had once bragged that someone would name a candy bar for him if he played in the Big Apple. He now had the chance to see if his prediction would be fulfilled.

Mr. October

Unfortunately, Jackson got off on the wrong foot with the Yankees. Comments he made in an interview in *Sport* magazine suggested that he thought he was the most important player on the team. Reggie expounded, "You know this team . . . it all flows from me. I've got to keep it going. I'm the straw that stirs the drink. It all comes back to me."[76] This attitude immediately alienated many of his new teammates.

Jackson made the situation worse during the team's first press conference of the spring. Fondling his bat, Jackson said, "You see this? This is the Dues Collector. This now helps the Yankees intimidate every other team in baseball. Nobody will

Jackson's love of the cameras often got him in trouble with his teammates.

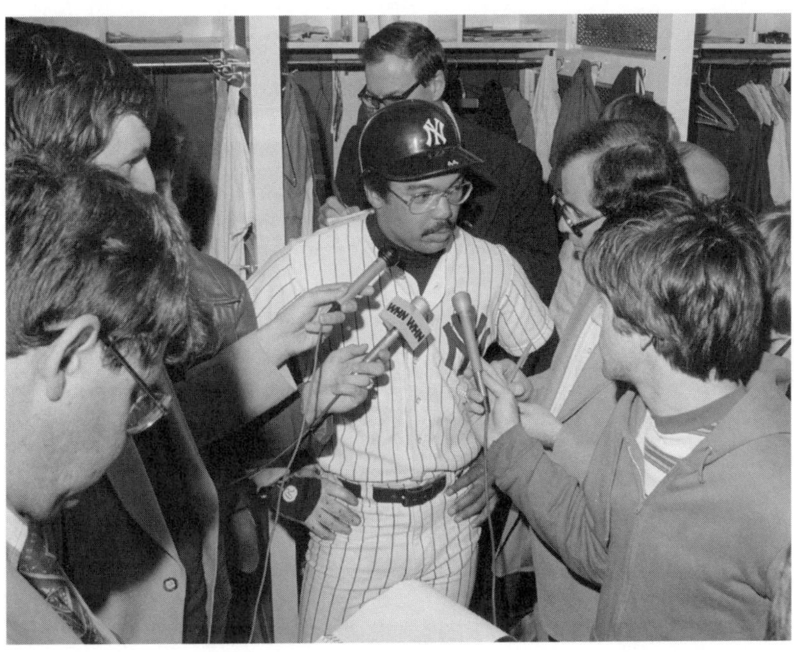

embarrass the Yankees in the World Series as long as I am carrying the Dues Collector."[77]

Jackson was able to overcome some of the resentment these comments earned him by putting together a solid 1977 season. He clouted 32 home runs, drove home a team-leading 110 runs, and finished third in the league in slugging average with a mark of .550. Winning over manager Billy Martin, however, was another matter altogether.

When Martin had been a player, he had fought for every possible advantage. He gave 100 percent at all times, making the most of his limited athletic ability. As a manager, he insisted on the same attitude from his players. During a game against the Red Sox that June, Martin thought Jackson had loafed on one play in which he went after a fly ball in the outfield. Martin sent Paul Blair in to replace his star and Jackson returned to the dugout in a rage. The manager confronted him as television cameras recorded and broadcast the scene nationally.

Jackson publicly complained that racism was at the heart of Martin's attitude toward him. "It makes me cry the way they treat me on this team. The Yankee pinstripes are Ruth and Gehrig and DiMaggio and Mantle. I'm just a black man to them who doesn't know how to be subservient."[78] The controversy eventually subsided, but the ill will between the two men lingered. Fellow Yankee and former Athletics teammate Hunter understood that the problem was both Jackson's and the Yankees'. "The difference with the Yankees," he said, "is guys paid attention to what he said. At Oakland nobody listened to him. We just watched him hit." Hunter went on, "Reggie's really a good guy. . . . He'd give you the shirt off his back. Of course, he'd call a press conference to announce it."[79]

In spite of the team's internal squabbles, New York won the East Division title, then defeated the Kansas City Royals in the League Championship Series. In Game 6 of the World Series against the Los Angeles Dodgers, Jackson put on an incredible show. After walking on four pitches his first time at bat, he hit the first pitch he saw from Burt Hooton for a two-run homer in the fourth inning. His next time up, he faced relief pitcher Elias Sosa and again hit the first pitch for a home run. When he came to the plate in the eighth, the Yankees held a 7-4 lead. With

Charlie Hough on the mound, Reggie hit the first pitch he saw into the centerfield bleachers. Three pitches, three swings, three home runs. Even the Dodgers were impressed. "I must admit," said Los Angeles first baseman Steve Garvey, "when Reggie hit his third homer and I was sure nobody was looking, I applauded in my glove."[80] All told, Jackson hit five home runs in the Series, scored ten runs, drove home eight, batted .450, and compiled a slugging average of 1.250. It was one of the greatest Series performances of all time and earned Jackson his second Series Most Valuable Player award.

Later that fall, one of Jackson's brashest predictions was fulfilled when Clark Candy launched the Reggie bar. Jackson had become the first baseball player to have a candy bar named after him. (Contrary to popular belief, the Baby Ruth bar was not named after Babe Ruth, but rather after President Grover Cleveland's young daughter.) With tongue in cheek, many suggested the confection was just like its namesake: sweet and nutty. Catfish Hunter took his own gentle poke at his teammate: "When you unwrap a Reggie bar," said Hunter, "it tells you how good it is."[81]

The Yankees followed a similar pattern in 1978. In July, Jackson and Martin clashed on the field, this time during a game against Kansas City. With Reggie at bat, Martin signaled for a bunt, then changed his mind and canceled the order. Jackson tried to bunt anyway, and struck out. For his defiance of Martin's orders, Jackson was suspended for five games. Martin complained about Jackson and team owner Steinbrenner, whose meddling Martin resented, to a sportswriter from the *New York Times:* "One's a born liar [Jackson] and the other's convicted [Steinbrenner]."[82] (This was a reference to an illegal contribution Steinbrenner had made to former president Richard Nixon's 1972 campaign.) For his comment, Martin was fired.

The Yankees rallied around new skipper Bob Lemon. After making a sensational comeback during the regular season to catch Boston, they defeated the Red Sox in a one-game playoff for the division crown. They again bested Kansas City in the League Championship Series, with Jackson batting an incredible .462. Their World Series opponent again was the Dodgers.

Jackson overcame some of his teammates' resentment by having a solid season in 1977 and by achieving one of the greatest World Series performances of all time.

Jackson did not duplicate his batting feats of 1977, but he still hit .391, with a pair of homers and eight RBI. He played an instrumental part in the Yankees victory, however, particularly in the pivotal Game 4. With the Dodgers leading 3-1, Jackson was hit by shortstop Bill Russell's throw to first in an attempt to complete a double play that would have ended the inning. The Yankees' second run scored on the play, despite Dodger protests that Jackson should have been called out on interference for intentionally throwing his hip at the ball. New York tied the score in the eighth inning, then won in the tenth to tie the Series at two games apiece. The Yankees ran over the Dodgers in the next two games to win their twenty-second world championship.

Despite a .297 average and 29 home runs from Jackson, New York dropped to third place in 1979. They bounced back with an East Division title in 1980, with Reggie batting .300 for the only time in his career. He also drilled 41 homers to lead the league for the third time, and drove home 111 runs.

The fifth and final year of Jackson's contract was 1981. In the strike-shortened season, the Yankees made the playoffs, but could not advance past the League Championship Series. At age thirty-five, Reggie batted only .237, with 15 homers and 54 runs batted in. Steinbrenner's advisers told him that Jackson was washed up. When Reggie filed for free agency following the end of the season, Steinbrenner allowed him to leave. "Mr. October's" tenure in New York City had come to an end.

Back to the West Coast

Despite Steinbrenner's calculations, Jackson was not yet finished. He signed with the California Angels and enjoyed five seasons with the team. He tied for the American League lead in home runs for the fourth time in 1982, blasting thirty- nine. The Angels won a West Division title that year, and another in 1986. Following that campaign, Jackson returned to the Oakland Athletics for one final season. After batting just .220 for the A's, Reggie hung up his spikes at age forty-one.

Jackson's career record includes 563 home runs, good for sixth place on the all-time list. He also had a record .755 slugging average in World Series play, together with a .357 batting mark, 10 home runs, and 24 RBI. On the other side of the ledger, Jackson also struck out a record 2,597 times in his career, 661 more than anyone else.

Since his retirement, Jackson has been a consultant with the Yankees as the team's special assignment assistant of baseball

Jackson played his fifth and final year with the Yankees in 1981.

operations. He spends time with the team in Florida every year during spring training, and works closely with George Steinbrenner. Reggie also has his own sports memorabilia company, and is a spokesman for a computer firm and telecommunications company. In his spare time, he collects vintage automobiles.

Reggie was elected to the Hall of Fame in 1993, his first year of eligibility. Despite having spent ten years of his career with the Athletics, his plaque at Cooperstown shows him wearing a Yankees cap. New York City was the only town big enough for "Mr. October."

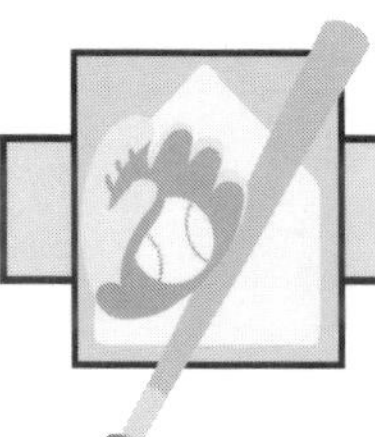

CHAPTER 8

Derek Jeter

Derek Jeter knew he wanted to be a New York Yankee by the time he was eight years old. Many youngsters harbor similar fantasies, but the overwhelming majority never see them through to fruition; Jeter is one who has. His talent carried him from the ballfields of Michigan to the most famous ballpark of all, Yankee Stadium in New York City. Not only has he realized his dream, he has far exceeded it.

At an age when many players are still struggling to make a name for themselves at the major league level, Jeter has established himself while playing for the most famous baseball team in the

Derek Jeter had wanted to be a Yankee since he was eight years old.

world, under intense media scrutiny. His talent, determination, good looks, and winning personality have made him one of the brightest young stars to come along in years.

Destined to Be a Yankee

Major General Abner Doubleday, mythologized as the inventor of baseball, was born on June 26, 1819. Exactly 155 years later, in 1974, Derek Sanderson Jeter was born in Pequannock, New Jersey. His father, Charles, who is black, was a drug and alcohol abuse counselor, and his mother, Dorothy, who is white, an accountant. Derek lived in West Milford, New Jersey, until he was four, when the family, which included younger sister Sharlee, moved to Kalamazoo, Michigan. Derek still returned to New Jersey each summer, however, to stay with his grandparents.

On one of these visits, Derek's grandmother, Dorothy Connors, took him to see the Yankees play. From that day on, his dream in life was to play ball for the Bronx Bombers. He looked forward to his summer vacation, when he would have a chance to see his favorite player, Dave Winfield, perform. He kept hold of his dream, even while living in Michigan. He went so far as to predict his future occupation in his eighth-grade yearbook from St. Augustine's Elementary School.

Jeter was encouraged to follow his dreams by his parents. They urged him to do his best in everything he tried, from athletics to schoolwork, and supported him every step of the way. His fierce determination to succeed is one of the qualities that sets him apart from others.

Jeter's biracial heritage was never a problem for him. He got along well with friends of all races, and could not understand why anyone would think less of him because of his background. Derek was taught to be cautious of people, but to treat everyone the same. He understood that it was better not to be upset by other people's ignorance, but rather to try to learn from it. His involvement in sports also helped him to accept others, no matter what their race or nationality.

Derek starred in both baseball and basketball at Kalamazoo Central High School. He batted .557 as a junior and .508 in his senior year, when he was named the 1992 high school player of the year by the American Baseball Coaches Association. Scouts for Cincinnati told him he would be drafted by the Reds with the fifth pick of the amateur draft that year. The Reds changed their minds at the last minute, however, and the Yankees picked him next, the first high school player to be chosen. Jeter signed his first professional contract two days after his eighteenth birthday, for a package worth $800,000.

Jeter reported to the Yankees Tampa farm team, but struggled in his first professional season. He batted .210, splitting time between Class A teams in Tampa and Greensboro. Looking back on those times, he reflects, "I expected the competition to be as good as it was, but I thought I'd do better."[83] The next year at Greensboro, he raised his average to .295. By 1994, it became obvious that he was a player to watch. He batted a combined .344 with Tampa, Albany, and the Yankees Triple A farm club at Columbus. For his performance, he was named minor league player of the year by *Baseball America*, the *Sporting News*, and *USA Today Baseball Weekly*. He was on his way to another fine season at Columbus in 1995 when he was called up to the Yankees early in the season. He made his major league debut on May 29, going hitless in an 8-7 loss to the Seattle Mariners. He batted .250 in fifteen games for the big league club before being sent back down to the minors for additional seasoning. He would be back to stay in 1996.

The Big City

In spring training that year, Jeter impressed everyone who saw him, including Yankees owner George Steinbrenner. "We'll be patient with him," promised the boss. "Every year you look for Derek Jeter to stumble, and he just doesn't. He dominated rookie ball, so we moved him to [Class] A and he dominated there. We sent him to Double A, and he dominated there. At Columbus it was the same thing. I'm telling you, he could be one of the special ones."[84]

When Jeter made the opening day lineup that year, he became the first rookie shortstop to do so for the Yankees since Tom Tresh with the 1962 club. In his second time at bat, facing veteran hurler Dennis Martinez of the Cleveland Indians, Jeter cracked his first major league homer. He continued his solid play, and expectations began to rise. The players, however, realized it was important to go slowly, even if that could be difficult in the Big Apple. "I think patience is the key," said veteran third baseman Wade Boggs. "But we're in New York. Patience and New York don't always go together."[85]

In Jeter's case, the worries proved to be unfounded. He showed maturity far beyond his years, batting .314, scoring 104 runs, hitting 10 homers, driving in 78 runs, and stealing 14 bases. The Yankees won the American League East by four games, defeated the Texas Rangers in the AL Division Series, and beat the Baltimore Orioles in the AL Championship Series.

In the first game of the Baltimore series, Jeter got one of the most controversial hits in postseason history. With the Yankees trailing 4-3 in the eighth inning, Jeter hit a long fly ball to deep

In 1996, Jeter became the first rookie shortstop to make the opening day lineup since 1962.

right field. Just as Orioles outfielder Tony Tarasco was getting ready to make the catch, a twelve-year-old fan reached over the fence and caught the ball. Despite Baltimore protests that Jeter should have been out because of fan interference, the umpires called the hit a home run and the game was tied. The Yankees went on to win on an eleventh-inning home run by Bernie Williams.

Jeter's performance under the pressure of the playoffs impressed manager Joe Torre: "You always want to lean on experienced players in the postseason. But Derek doesn't see the postseason as something different."[86]

After disposing of Baltimore, New York moved on to play the Atlanta Braves in the World Series. The Yankees defeated the Braves in an exciting six-game affair to win the twenty-third championship in their glorious history. Derek again played an important role in the team's success. His batting average for the postseason was .361, with 22 hits in 61 at bats.

In addition to getting a championship ring in his first big league season, Jeter also won the American League Rookie of the Year Award. The media came after him like flies to honey. Everyone wanted to interview the handsome, twenty-two-year-old shortstop. It was a memorable year, but Derek was able to keep things in perspective. "I really think I am getting this attention because I'm the youngest guy on the team," he would say. "I find it hard to believe. I'm just an average guy who plays baseball for a living."[87]

The next year, the Yankees finished second in the AL East and were defeated by the Cleveland Indians in the AL Division Series. Jeter's batting average dipped to .291, but he did score 116 runs. He continued his postseason heroics, hitting a pair of home runs while batting .333 against Cleveland. After winning the championship the year before, 1997 was a disappointment to Jeter and Yankee fans. No one could have predicted what lay in store for 1998.

A Year for the Ages

When the Yankees reported for spring training that year, they were determined to make it back to the World Series. They quickly jumped into first place in the American League East.

They kept winning and opened up a lead that was never threatened. They clinched first place and didn't let up. By the time the season was over, the Yankees had won an American League record 114 games against only 48 losses. They finished 22 games ahead of the second-place Red Sox.

Batting second in the batting order, Jeter excelled in every phase of the game. He turned in career highs in nearly every offensive category, including hits, runs scored, triples, home runs, runs batted in, and stolen bases. Always a good fielder, he committed only nine errors, half his previous low.

Entering postseason play, the 1998 Yankees were making a solid claim as one of the greatest teams of all time. To be ranked among the greats, however, they would have to win a championship.

They began their quest by demolishing the Texas Rangers in three straight games in the League Division Series. Next, they defeated Cleveland in six games in the League Championship Series. The final obstacle was the National League champion San Diego Padres in the World Series.

Jeter impressed everyone by excelling in all areas of play.

San Diego proved to be no match for the Bronx Bombers. The New Yorkers won four straight games to take the championship. After struggling in the first two rounds, Jeter bounced back in the Series. He batted .353 against San Diego, collecting six hits in seventeen at bats. Once again, the Series brought out the best in the emerging superstar.

No one could deny that the 1998 club was one of baseball's all-time great teams.

Including postseason play, they won an unprecedented 125 games against only 50 losses. It would have been only natural for the next year to be a letdown.

Manager Joe Torre would not allow that, however, and neither would the players' pride. New York won 98 games to take another East Division crown. Incredibly, Jeter again surpassed his previous career highs in nearly every offensive department. In 158 games, he scored 134 runs and tallied 219 hits, 37 doubles, 9 triples, 24 home runs, 102 runs batted in, a batting average of .349, and a slugging percentage of .552.

In the postseason, both Jeter and the Yankees continued to impress the entire baseball world. The team won 11 games out of 12. Jeter again rose to the occasion. He batted .375, with 18 hits in 48 postseason at bats. By defeating the Atlanta Braves in the World Series, the Yankees had won three championships in the four seasons since Jeter had taken over the shortstop position. His superb all-around play had won over both his teammates and opposing players and managers. As St. Louis Cardinals manager Tony LaRussa explained, "The key to being a really good player [at shortstop], besides having the tools, is to have a sense for the game. . . . You [have to] understand when you have to charge the ball—all the little things. And Jeter has a great sense for the game."[88]

The Subway Series

The Yankees' 2000 season was more challenging than the previous two. They clinched the American League East, but slumped at season's end. They lost fifteen of their final eighteen games, including their last seven in a row. Jeter, however, surpassed the two-hundred hit level for the third season in a row, batting .339 to lead the team. Earlier in the year, he had added to his accomplishments by being named the Most Valuable Player of the all-star game. He had three hits in that contest, including a double, and drove home a pair of runs in the American League's 6-3 victory. Jeter was the first Yankee ever honored as the game's MVP. "It means a lot," said Jeter. "At the shortstop position in the American League, you don't know if you're going to get a chance to come to an All-Star Game, let alone star in one. You don't want to take it for granted."[89]

Jeter holds up his Most Valuable Player award for his performance in the 2000 World Series.

In the American League Division Series, New York's slump continued as the Oakland A's won Game 1 by a score of 5-3. The Yankees bounced back, however, taking three of the next four games to advance into the League Championship Series. Jeter struggled against Oakland's young pitching staff, collecting just four singles in nineteen at bats.

The League Championship Series followed a similar pattern. The Yankees dropped the first game against the Seattle Mariners, then won the next three in a row. After Seattle salvaged Game 5, New York won the next contest to take the pennant. Derek's bat perked up in the second game. Along with a single, he had a two-run homer. In Game 4, his three-run homer in the fifth inning opened the scoring in a 5-0 Yankees win. All told, Jeter batted .333 against Seattle, with 6 hits in 18 at bats.

The New York Mets were the Yankees' opponent in the first "Subway Series" since 1956. Jeter was unquestionably the key performer, playing an important role in each of the four Yankees' victories. His performance was all the more impressive when the conditions surrounding the Series are considered. Even though the Yankees had won three championships in the previous four years, this Series was special because the crosstown Mets were the opponents. Jeter knew the Yankees had to win or lose the loyalty of the fans. "We had a lot to lose," he would later say. "I would have moved right out of the city if we'd lost. You could have taken our three [World Series] rings and thrown them out the window, as far as Yankees fans were concerned."[90]

In Game 1, his off-balance relay throw nailed Mets outfielder Timo Perez at the plate as he tried to score in the sixth inning.

Jeter also had a single, a walk, and scored a run. In Game 2, Jeter had three hits, including a pair of doubles, and scored a run. He had two more hits and another run scored in the Mets victory in Game 3.

For Game 4, Joe Torre moved Jeter into the leadoff position in the batting order, up from his customary number-two spot. In response, the young shortstop hit the first pitch of the game from Bobby Jones into the left-field seats for a home run. He

In Game Four of the 2000 World Series, Jeter hit a home run on the first pitch of the first inning.

tripled his next time up, and scored what proved to be the winning run in the Yanks' 3-2 win. In the Series finale, he hit another homer in the sixth inning to tie the score at 2-2. The Yankees won their third consecutive championship when they scored a pair of runs in the ninth inning.

For his heroics, Jeter was named the Most Valuable Player of the Series. He batted .409, with nine hits in twenty-two at bats, and extended his Series hitting streak to fourteen consecutive games, third-longest of all time. Derek's position on the team was now obvious to everyone. "The guy's incredible," said reliever Mike Stanton. "I don't think there's any doubt. He's the leader of this team."[91]

A Hint of Things to Come

With four World Series rings in his first five seasons, Jeter has put together a record that ranks with that of other Yankee legends. Joe DiMaggio, for example, also won four titles in his first five years. Over that period, both Jeter and DiMaggio played in nineteen Series games, with their teams each winning sixteen. The Yankee Clipper hit more home runs and drove home more runs than the young shortstop, but Jeter has outhit the center fielder, .342 to .304.

In February 2001, George Steinbrenner guaranteed that Jeter would remain an integral part of the the Yankees in the future. He signed his shortstop to a ten-year contract for an incredible $189 million. Jeter would have been eligible for free agency after the 2001 season, but had no intention of leaving the Yankees family. "I never intended to play elsewhere," he revealed, "and to be honest with you, never intended to look elsewhere."[92] For that, Yankees fans can be especially grateful.

Jeter realizes he has had much for which to be grateful. He was inspired by his idol, former Yankee Dave Winfield, to start the Turn 2 Foundation in 1996. The foundation was established to help support and create activities and programs to motivate high-risk youths to turn away from drugs and alcohol and choose healthy lifestyles. In this way, he has been able to help thousands of needy kids.

Jeter has improved himself at every step in his career, honing his skills and utilizing his talents to the best of his ability. The

Jeter's exceptional talents will likely carry him to the Baseball Hall of Fame.

degree to which he has succeeded can be seen in the words of praise from Yankees opponents, such as Texas Rangers manager Johnny Oates. "Jeter is a six-tool player," gushed Oates. "I've never eaten with him so I can't tell you if he has good table manners, but I would imagine he has those too."[93]

At this point, where his talents will carry him is a matter of conjecture. As owner Steinbrenner has said, "I can't think of any player who is more exceptional than Derek Jeter. All the things that you'd want a player to be, he is. He does it on the field and off the field."[94] His potential seems unlimited. His popularity with fans (particularly young girls) has never been higher. If he continues along the same track, it is likely his journey will one day take him to the Baseball Hall of Fame in Cooperstown, New York.

Notes

Introduction: A Tough Team for a Tough Town

1. Quoted in Editor & Publisher Online, Print Press Briefs, August 21, 1998, www.mediainfo.com/ephome/news/newshtm/nuggets/brfs082198.htm.

Chapter 1: The Making of A Dynasty

2. Quoted in Mark Gallagher, *The Yankee Encyclopedia*. New York: Leisure Press, 1982, p. 350.
3. Quoted in Gallagher, *The Yankee Encyclopedia*, p. 358.
4. Quoted in Gallagher, *The Yankee Encyclopedia*, p. 382.
5. Quoted in William Ladson, "Boss Talk," in Editors of the Sporting News, *The Yankees: Steinbrenner's 25 Years of Triumph and Turmoil*, 1998, p. 22.
6. Quoted in Rob Parker, "He Likes Me, He Likes Me Not," in Editors of the Sporting News, *The Yankees: Steinbrenner's 25 Years of Triumph and Turmoil*, 1998, p. 121.
7. Quoted in Peter Schmuck, "Going Down," in Editors of the Sporting News, *The Yankees: Steinbrenner's 25 Years of Triumph and Turmoil*, 1998, p. 68.
8. Quoted in Joe Gergen, "The Feud," in Editors of the Sporting News, *The Yankees: Steinbrenner's 25 Years of Triumph and Turmoil*, 1998, p. 74.
9. Quoted in Gergen, "The Feud," in Editors of the Sporting News, *The Yankees: Steinbrenner's 25 Years of Triumph and Turmoil*, 1998, p. 75.

Chapter 2: Babe Ruth

10. Quoted in Paul Adomites and Saul Wisnia, *Babe Ruth: His Life and Times*. Lincolnwood, IL: Publications International, 1995, p. 24.
11. Quoted in Frederick G. Lieb, "Remembering the Babe,"

Sporting News, August 25, 1948, tsn.sportingnews.com/archives/baseball/92580.html.

12. Quoted in David Pietrusza, Matthew Silverman, and Michael Gershman, eds., *Baseball: The Biographical Encyclopedia*. New York: Total/Sports Illustrated, 2000, p. 985.
13. Quoted in Robert W. Creamer, *Babe: The Legend Comes to Life*. New York: Simon and Schuster, 1974, p. 148.
14. Quoted in Glenn Liebman, *Yankee Shorts*. Chicago: Contemporary Books, 1997, p. 5.
15. Quoted in Gallagher, *The Yankee Encyclopedia*, p. 578.
16. Quoted in Lieb, "Remembering the Babe," *Sporting News*.
17. Quoted in Lieb, "Remembering the Babe," *Sporting News*.
18. Quoted in Lieb, "Remembering the Babe," *Sporting News*.
19. Quoted in Lieb, "Remembering the Babe," *Sporting News*.
20. Quoted in The Official Babe Ruth Web Site, www.baberuth.com/quote2a.html.

Chapter 3: Lou Gehrig

21. Quoted in Joseph J. Vecchione, ed., *The New York Times Book of Sports Legends*. New York: Random House, 1991, p. 68.
22. Quoted in Larry Schwartz, "More on the 'Iron Horse,'" ESPN.com Classic, September 21, 2000, espn.go.com/classic/s/000809lougehrigadd.html.
23. Quoted in Dave Hensel, "Lou Gehrig '25: Larrupin' Lou of Columbia U.,'" *Daily Spectator*, January 19, 2000, 209.35.163.234/special/sports99/athletes1.htm.
24. Quoted in Vecchione, *The New York Times Book of Sports Legends*. New York: Random House, p. 71.
25. Quoted in Pietrusza, Silverman, and Gershman, *Baseball*, p. 402.
26. Quoted in Larry Schwartz, "Gehrig Legacy One of Irony," ESPN.com Classic, espn.go.com/sportscentury/features/00014204.html.
27. Quoted in Pietrusza, Silverman, and Gershman, *Baseball*, p. 404.
28. Quoted in James G. Robinson, "The Iron Horse's Last Game," CBS Sportsline: The Baseball Online Library, web2.sportsline.com/u/baseball/bol/features/flashbacks/04_30_1939.html.

29. Quoted in Robinson, "The Iron Horse's Last Game."
30. Quoted in CMG Worldwide, "Lou Gehrig Biography," www.cmgww.com/baseball/gehrig/bio2.html.
31. Quoted in Vecchione, *The New York Times Book of Sports Legends*, p. 75.
32. Quoted in CMG Worldwide, "Lou Gehrig Biography."

Chapter 4: Joe DiMaggio

33. Quoted in Paul Dottino and Thomas J. Fitzgerald, "Joe D: A Legend Lost," *Bergen Record*, March 9, 1999, www.bergen.com/yankees/jdobitfi199903091.htm.
34. Quoted in Larry Schwartz, "SportsCentury Biography of Joe DiMaggio," ESPN.com Classic, July 25, 1999, espn.go.com/classic/000706joedimaggio.html.
35. Quoted in MSNBC Sports, "DiMaggio Chronology," msnbc.com/modules/sports/dimaggio/default.asp.
36. Quoted in Liebman, *Yankee Shorts*, p. 112.
37. Quoted in The Editors of Beckett Publications, *Joe DiMaggio: The Yankee Clipper*. Dallas: Beckett, 1998, p. 9.
38. Quoted in Editors of Beckett Publications, *Joe DiMaggio*, p. 10.
39. Quoted in Paul Dottino, "A Man with Amazing Grace," *Bergen Record*, March 9, 1999. www.bergen.com/yankees/clipper09199903092.htm.
40. Quoted in Editors of Beckett Publications, *Joe DiMaggio*, p. 27.
41. Quoted in Liebman, *Yankee Shorts*, p. 113.
42. Quoted in Editors of Beckett Publications, *Joe DiMaggio*, pp. 82–83.
43. Quoted in John F. Yarbrough, "Joltin' Joe DiMaggio: Yankee Clipper Inspired a Nation," ABCNews, www.abcnews.go.com/sections/sports/DailyNews/dimaggio990722.html.
44. Quoted in Editors of Beckett Publications, *Joe DiMaggio*, p. 85.
45. Quoted in Lee Green, *Sportswit*. New York: Fawcett Crest, 1984, p. 4.
46. Quoted in Kevin Fitzpatrick, "A Nation's Sad Eyes," FOX Sports Online, March 8, 1999, www.bway.net/~kfitz/writing14.htm.
47. Rudolph W. Giuliani, "Remarks at Joe DiMaggio's Memorial

Service," The Official New York City Web Site, April 23, 1999, www.ci.nyc.ny.us/html/om/html/99a/dimaggio2.html.

Chapter 5: Casey Stengel

48. Quoted in CMG Worldwide, "The Official Casey Stengel Web Site," www.cmgww.com/baseball/stengel/index.html.
49. Quoted in Vecchione, *The New York Times Book of Sports Legends,* p. 327.
50. Quoted in Vecchione, *The New York Times Book of Sports Legends,* p. 327.
51. Quoted in Pietrusza, Silverman, and Gershman, *Baseball,* p. 1,081.
52. Quoted in The Baseball Online Library, cbs.sportsline.com/u/baseball/bol/ballplayers/S/Stengel_Casey.html.
53. Quoted in Pietrusza, Silverman, and Gershman, *Baseball,* p. 1,081.
54. Quoted in Vecchione, *The New York Times Book of Sports Legends,* p. 330.
55. Quoted in Vecchione, *The New York Times Book of Sports Legends,* p. 328.
56. Quoted in The Baseball Online Library.
57. Quoted in The Baseball Online Library.
58. Quoted in Vecchione, *The New York Times Book of Sports Legends,* p. 329.
59. Quoted in Robert W. Creamer, *Stengel: His Life and Times.* New York: Fireside Books, 1984, p. 332.

Chapter 6: Mickey Mantle

60. Quoted in Pietrusza, Silverman, and Gershman, *Baseball,* p. 704.
61. Quoted in Pietrusza, Silverman, and Gershman, *Baseball,* p. 704.
62. Quoted in Pietrusza, Silverman, and Gershman, *Baseball,* p. 704.
63. Quoted in The Official Mickey Mantle Web Site, www.themick.com/MickeyQuotes.htm.
64. Quoted in *Mantle Remembered.* New York: Warner Books, 1995, p. 14.

65. Quoted in Pietrusza, Silverman, and Gershman, *Baseball*, p. 705.
66. Quoted in *Mantle Remembered*, p. 53.
67. Quoted in Baseball Almanac, "Quotations: Mickey Mantle," baseball-almanac.com/quomant.shtml.
68. Quoted in *Mantle Remembered*, p. 79.
69. Quoted in Tribute to Mickey Mantle, "Quotes," www.theswearingens.com/mick/quotes.htm.
70. Quoted in Pietrusza, Silverman, and Gershman, *Baseball*, p. 705.
71. Quoted in Green, *Sportswit*, p. 139.

Chapter 7: Reggie Jackson

72. Quoted in Barry Mandell, "A Look Back: Reggie Jackson's Three Consecutive World Series Home Runs, 1977," Sports Map News Services, www.sportsmapnews.com/aa030.htm.
73. Quoted in Monte Poole, "Reggie Jackson, No. 25," *Celebrate 2000-ANG Newspapers*, January 13, 2001, www.celebrate2000-ang.com/sportsfigures.asp?Sports=Reggie_Jackson.
74. Quoted in Poole, "Reggie Jackson," *Celebrate 2000-ANG Newspapers*.
75. Quoted in Poole, "Reggie Jackson," *Celebrate 2000-ANG Newspapers*.
76. Quoted in Mandell, "A Look Back," Sports Map News Services.
77. Quoted in Mandell, "A Look Back," Sports Map News Services.
78. Quoted in Michael Adler, "Billy & Reggie's Brouhaha," CBS Sportsline: The Baseball Online Library, web2.sportsline.com/u/baseball/bol/features/flashbacks/06_18_1977.html.
79. Quoted in Mandell, "A Look Back," Sports Map News Services.
80. Quoted in Gallagher, *The Yankee Encyclopedia*, p. 457.
81. Quoted in Baseball Almanac, baseball-almanac.com/quojackr.shtml.
82. Quoted in Pietrusza, Silverman, and Gershman, *Baseball*, p. 551.

Chapter 8: Derek Jeter

83. Quoted in Sports Illustrated/CNN, "Timeline Derek Jeter," sportsillustrated.cnn.com/baseball/mlb/features/jeter/timeline.

84. Quoted in Gerry Callahan, "New York . . . New York," Sports Illustrated/CNN, May 6, 2000, sportsillustrated.cnn.com/features/cover/news/2000/10/26/jeter_flashback2/.
85. Quoted in Callahan, "New York . . . New York," Sports Illustrated/CNN.
86. Quoted in Kelly Whiteside, "Born to Be a Bomber," Sports Illustrated/CNN, November 13, 1996, sportsillustrated.cnn.com/features/cover/news/2000/10/26/jeter_flashback4.
87. Quoted in Sports Illustrated/CNN, "Timeline Derek Jeter."
88. Quoted in David Lennon, "Quality Kid," Editors of the Sporting News, *The Yankees: Steinbrenner's 25 Years of Triumph and Turmoil*, 1998, p. 99.
89. Quoted in Seth Livingstone, "AL Thrives on Young Bats, Old Arms," *USA Today Baseball Weekly*, July 13–18, 2000, p. 22.
90. Quoted in Tom Verducci, "The Toast of the Town," *Sports Illustrated*, November 6, 2000, p. 66.
91. Quoted in Sports Illustrated/CNN, "Season Sweep," October 27, 2000, sportsillustrated.cnn.com/baseball/mlb/2000/world_series/news/2000/10/26/jetermvp_ap.
92. Quoted in Sports Illustrated/CNN, "Derek's Dollars," February 9, 2001, sportsillustrated.cnn.com/baseball/mlb/news/2001/02/09/yankees_jeter_ap.
93. Quoted in The Baseball Online Library, "Derek Jeter," cbs.sportsline.com/u/baseball/bol/ballplayers/J/Jeter_Derek.html.
94. Quoted in Derek Jeter with Jack Curry, *The Life You Imagine*. New York: Crown, 2000, p. 15.

For Further Reading

Bill Madden and Moss Klein, *Damned Yankees*. New York: Warner, 1991. A behind-the-scenes look at the Yankees under George Steinbrenner's ownership.

John Mosedale, *The Greatest of All: The 1927 Yankees*. New York: Warner, 1975. A detailed history of what is generally accepted as baseball's greatest team of all time.

Ray Robinson and Christopher Jennison, *Yankee Stadium*. New York: Penguin Studio, 1998. A lavishly illustrated volume detailing the history of the most famous sports stadium in the country.

Gene Schoor, *The Illustrated History of Mickey Mantle*. New York: Carroll & Graf, 1996. The history of one of baseball's superstars, told through words and photos.

Mike Shatzkin, ed., *The Ballplayers*. New York: Arbor House, 1990. This volume contains entries on more than six thousand baseball players, teams, umpires, owners, writers, ballparks, and more.

Works Consulted

Books

Paul Adomites and Saul Wisnia, *Babe Ruth: His Life and Times.* Lincolnwood, IL: Publications International, 1995. The incredible story of Babe Ruth, issued on the one hundredth anniversary of his birth.

Maury Allen, *You Could Look It Up: The Life of Casey Stengel.* New York: Times Books, 1979. The biography of baseball's goodwill ambassador, and one of the greatest managers of all-time.

Robert W. Creamer, *Babe: The Legend Comes to Life.* New York: Simon and Schuster, 1974. The first full, in-depth biography about perhaps the most famous figure in American sports history.

Robert W. Creamer, *Stengel: His Life and Times.* New York: Fireside Books, 1984. An in-depth biography of baseball's greatest goodwill ambassador.

Joe DiMaggio, *Lucky to Be a Yankee.* New York: Grosset & Dunlap, 1951. The autobiography of the Yankee Clipper.

The Editors of Beckett Publications, *Joe DiMaggio: The Yankee Clipper.* Dallas: Beckett, 1998. A lavishly illustrated volume examining the career of Joe DiMaggio through articles and essays.

Mark Gallagher, *The Yankee Encyclopedia.* New York: Leisure Press, 1982. This 640-page work is the ultimate source of information on the Yankees.

Patrick Giles, *Derek Jeter: Pride of the Yankees.* New York: St. Martin's, 1998. An unauthorized biography of one of baseball's hottest young players.

Lee Green, *Sportswit.* New York: Fawcett Crest, 1984. A collection of quotes on various aspects of sports.

Derek Jeter with Jack Curry, *The Life You Imagine.* New York:

Crown, 2000. Derek Jeter's personal story, along with his rules for achieving success in life.

Glenn Liebman, *Yankee Shorts*. Chicago: Contemporary Books, 1997. A collection of 501 humorous one-liners by, and about, the Yankees.

Mantle Remembered. New York: Warner Books, 1995. With an introduction by Robert W. Creamer, this book is a collection of articles on Mantle which appeared over the years in *Sports Illustrated* magazine.

Mickey Mantle with Herb Gluck, *The Mick*. New York: Jove Books, 1986. The autobiography of the Commerce Comet.

David Pietrusza, Matthew Silverman, and Michael Gershman, eds., *Baseball: The Biographical Encyclopedia*. New York: Total/Sports Illustrated, 2000. This volume contains essays on more than two thousand of the most talented players, managers, umpires, executives, and journalists associated with the game of baseball.

Editors of The Sporting News, *The Yankees: Steinbrenner's 25 Years of Triumph and Turmoil*, St. Louis: Times Mirror, 1998.

Joseph J. Vecchione, ed., *The New York Times Book of Sports Legends*. New York: Random House, 1991. Fifty of the greatest athletes of all time are brought to life through the words of some of the greatest journalists of all time.

Periodicals

Seth Livingstone, "AL Thrives on Young Bats, Old Arms," *USA Today Baseball Weekly*, July 13–18, 2000.

Tom Verducci, "The Toast of the Town," *Sports Illustrated*, November 6, 2000.

Internet Resources

Michael Adler, "Billy & Reggie's Brouhaha," CBS Sportsline: The Baseball Online Library, web2.sportsline.com/u/baseball/bol/features/flashbacks/06_18_1977.html.

Gerry Callahan, "New York . . . New York," Sports Illustrated/CNN, May 6, 2000, sportsillustrated.cnn.com/features/cover/news/2000/10/26/jeter_flashback2.

Paul Dottino, "A Man with Amazing Grace," *Bergen Record*, March 9, 1999, www.bergen.com/yankees/clipper09199903092.htm.

Paul Dottino and Thomas J. Fitzgerald, "Joe D: A Legend Lost," *Bergen Record*, March 9, 1999, www.bergen.com/yankees/jdobitfi199903091.htm.

Kevin Fitzpatrick, "A Nation's Sad Eyes," FOX Sports Online, March 8, 1999, www.bway.net/~kfitz/writing14.htm.

Rudolph W. Giuliani, "Remarks at Joe DiMaggio's Memorial Service," The Official New York City Web Site, April 23, 1999, www.ci.nyc.ny.us/html/om/html/99a/dimaggio2.html.

Dave Hensel, "Lou Gehrig '25: Larrupin' Lou of Columbia U.," *Daily Spectator*, January 19, 2000, 209.35.163.234/special/sports99/athletes1.htm.

Frederick G. Lieb, "Remembering the Babe," *Sporting News*, August 25, 1948, tsn.sportingnews.com/archives/baseball/92580.html.

Barry Mandell, "A Look Back: Reggie Jackson's Three Consecutive World Series Home Runs, 1977," Sports Map News Services, www.sportsmapnews.com/aa030.htm.

MSNBC Sports, "DiMaggio Chronology," msnbc.com/modules/sports/dimaggio/default.asp.

Monte Poole, "Reggie Jackson, No. 25," *Celebrate 2000-ANG Newspapers*, January 13, 2001, www.celebrate2000-ang.com/sportsfigures.asp?Sports=Reggie_Jackson.

James G. Robinson, "The Iron Horse's Last Game," CBS Sportsline: The Baseball Online Library, web2.sportsline.com/u/baseball/bol/features/flashbacks/04_30_1939.html.

Larry Schwartz, "Gehrig Legacy One of Irony," ESPN.com Classic, espn.go.com/sportscentury/features/00014204.html.

Larry Schwartz, "More on the 'Iron Horse,'" ESPN.com Classic, September 21, 2000, espn.go.com/classic/s/000809lougehrigadd.html.

Larry Schwartz, "SportsCentury Biography of Joe DiMaggio," ESPN.com Classic, July 25, 1999, espn.go.com/classic/000706joedimaggio.html.

Kelly Whiteside, "Born to Be a Bomber," Sports Illustrated/

CNN, November 13, 1996, sportsillustrated.cnn.com/features/cover/news/2000/10/26/ jeter_flashback4.

John F. Yarbrough, "Joltin' Joe DiMaggio: Yankee Clipper Inspired a Nation," ABCNews, www.abcnews.go.com/sections/sports/DailyNews/dimaggio990722.html.

Websites

American National Biography Online (www.anb.org).

Baseball Almanac (baseball-almanac.com).

The Baseball Online Library (cbs.sportsline.com/u/baseball/bol).

CMG Worldwide, Inc. (www.cmgww.com).

Editor & Publisher Online (www.mediainfo.com).

The Official Babe Ruth Web Site (www.baberuth.com).

The Official Mickey Mantle Web Site (www.themick.com).

Sing 365 (www.sing365.com).

Sports Illustrated/CNN Web Site (sportsillustrated.cnn.com).

Tribute to Mickey Mantle (www.theswearingens.com/mick/index.html).

Index

Picture Credits

Cover Photo: © Al Bello/ALLSPORT
© AFP/CORBIS, 21
© Bettmann/CORBIS, 19, 28, 32, 39, 50, 59, 61, 69, 80, 81, 83, 91, 93
Brown Brothers, 10, 26, 37, 47, 55, 64, 67, 72, 77, 85
© CORBIS, 34
Culver Pictures, 46
© Duomo/CORBIS, 103, 105
FPG International, 11, 43
Hulton/Archive by Getty Images, 41, 57
Library of Congress, 23
Photofest, 18, 54, 75, 98
Photofest/Icon Archives, 15, 96
© Neal Preston/CORBIS, 88
© Reuters NewMedia Inc./CORBIS, 22, 100, 107, 108, 110
Joe Traver/Gamma Liaison/Archive, 52
© Underwood & Underwood/CORBIS, 13, 30

About the Author

John F. Grabowski is a native of Brooklyn, New York. He holds a bachelor's degree in psychology from City College of New York and a master's degree in educational psychology from Teacher's College, Columbia University. He has been a teacher for thirty-one years, as well as a freelance writer specializing in the fields of sports, education, and comedy. His body of published work includes twenty-eight books; a nationally syndicated sports column; consultation on several math textbooks; articles for newspapers, magazines, and the programs of professional sports teams; and comedy material sold to Jay Leno, Joan Rivers, Yakov Smirnoff, and numerous other comics. He and his wife, Patricia, live in Staten Island with their daughter, Elizabeth.